Kenny,

Fight On!

Money, Money, Everywhere - But Not a Drop for Main Street

Bob Eden

Money, Money, Everywhere - But Not a Drop for Main Street

10 Things You Need to Know to Get a Small Business Loan Today!

By

Bob Coleman

Published in the United States of America by Coleman Publishing

This book represents the views of the author. This book is presented for informational purposes only. The author does not promise you will get a loan. While every attempt has been made to verify the information in this book, the author does not assume any responsibility for errors, inaccuracies, or omissions.

www.colemanpublishing.com

Library of Congress Cataloging-in-Publication Data is available upon request.

ISBN 978-0-9833811-7-4

for my dad, Brooks Coleman;

my wife Cindy;

and the boys: Brooks, Joseph, and Michael.

Table of Contents

Part I:
Bank Think, Past and Present

Chapter 1: Main Street USA

Empty storefronts. A proliferation of "For Lease" signs everywhere. The scene repeats itself on every block. Throughout your town. On your Main Street. On everyone's Main Street. Throughout the country. Throughout the world.

We bailed out the economy. No—we bailed out Wall Street for $787 billion. That's $787 billion, with a "b." And this is what we get?

Million-dollar bonuses on Wall Street are back. The stock market is back. General Motors is making money. The Huffington Post is sold for $315 million. Economic growth, while not robust, is, well, growing.

Nice, but why is unemployment still high? Why are we close to 20% underemployed? Why do we have a generation of college graduates working at Starbucks?

Because the small business owner—the creator of jobs—can't get money and can't get a loan.

I'll repeat myself: Without credit and without loans, small business—Main Street—is not going to expand. It's not going to hire anyone.

The key to gauging economic growth is the employment numbers. When people have jobs they buy stuff. When they don't, they can't.

And they can't get a job if the creator of 67% of new jobs—the small business entrepreneur—can't get capital and can't get a loan.

Period.

In my hometown of La Cañada, California, as you drive up and down Main Street you can clearly see and understand the devastation the Great Recession has caused to the community. Everyone's community. This is a microeconomic book. (I still have problems grasping macroeconomics. My professors at USC gave me the grades to prove it!)

This is a discussion of credit and lending.

Small business credit. Small business loans, and how to get them. Small businesses and their bankers must understand the financial landscape has changed. Forever? Possibly. I don't know. Nobody does.

Let's just get through 2011 first.

In my view of microeconomics, how we extricate ourselves from the Great Recession is to rebuild America one store, one business, one job, one Main Street, and one community at a time.

How did we get here? Don't worry, this isn't a history book. There are some pretty cool books being written about that. I'll leave that to others.

I want to know how we get *out* of here.

Money, Money, Everywhere is a practical book.

It's a book about lending. Small business lending.

It's a book about how my clients think. The bankers. I write a weekly newsletter for bankers about the small business banking industry. They pay me for data, analysis, research, and trends.

I'm not talking about Wall Street bankers. They should be ashamed to call themselves bankers. Just call them vultures and parasites who take a commission for being in the right place in the right time.

They don't create anything. They destroy lives with bad judgment, bad products, and bad hair.

They get a taste, Tony Soprano-style. A cut of the action. I want to call them glorified used-car salesmen, but that isn't fair to used-car salesmen. Those people provide a real, valuable service to the country. Wall Street bankers don't.

I'm talking about small business bankers. Community bankers. I'm talking about those men and women who believe in Main Street and in community.

I'm talking about those who show up in the choir everyday doing God's work. To help the shopkeepers, the entrepreneurs, and the risk takers of Main Street.

Main Street creates the jobs. Main Street buys the goods and creates products and services for the community.

Money, Money, Everywhere is a book to help you understand today's banking thinking.

It really is a credit desert out there. Did you know that in the past several years banks have lopped off $1 trillion of credit card lines? (Small businesses' number one source of credit is the credit card, but more on that later.)

The closure of the home equity ATM, another critical source of small business financing, has dried up close to another $1 trillion of credit.

Add those two numbers together and they exceed the federal deficit.

Main Street Is a Disaster Zone

If a fire hit —as the Station Fire hit La Cañada and the mountains of the San Gabriels in 2009, one of the largest in U.S. history—or a hurricane, or an earthquake, the Feds would pour in billions of dollars for disaster recovery.

But not for the disaster on Main Street.

Because when one business fails, that isn't news. It's not sexy.

No one has bussed in hundreds of small business supporters from out of state to protest the closing of the local cafe.

No one is on TV talking about small business-busting moves by politicians causing the closing of the local bookstore. That owner never gave a dime to the politicians. He or she never networked with other small business owners to lobby for Main Street.

They were just working eighteen hours day to make a go of it, and certainly didn't have the time to play the political game of giving money and hosting fund raisers to their various politicians.

They worried about customers. They worried about sales. They worried if there was enough cash in the bank to pay the phone and electric bill, not who their Congressman was and whether there was a D or an R attached to the name.

If your Main Street is bolstered by the presence of a large employer (a GM plant or an Air Force base), and that employer announces an upcoming mass layoff, the entire community becomes obsessed with it. The mayor lobbies Congress to retain those jobs, the local chamber of commerce enacts a publicity campaign, and the negative impact of losing those several hundred jobs is understood.

That type of passion and commitment does not exist for mom-and-pop operators on Main Street.

Driving down your Main Street, you probably wouldn't even be aware of the financial devastation that has occurred; but in totality, the impact of those businesses closing can be greater than the impact of a mass plant layoff.

It is Main Street that keeps the community vibrant. The entrepreneurs who run mom-and-pop shops buy the Girl Scout cookies, sponsor little league baseball and youth soccer teams, and buy the scoreboard at the local high school football stadium. They live in the community and they invest in the community.

According to the Small Business Administration, for every dollar spent in a Main Street business, sixty cents is retained in the community. If you spend that dollar at a big-box store such as Wal-Mart, only twenty cents is retained (Want a source? Just Google it. There are plenty of stats there.).

In my opinion Wal-Mart has killed more small businesses than politicians possibly could have, even with their collective anti-small business agenda.

One of the casualties in La Cañada from the Great Recession was a local gift shop that had been in business since 1957. It quietly went under after supporting a family and numerous employees for all of those years.

After the closing, a poignant notice was taped to the front of the store: "Whether you shopped with us one day or sixty years, Thank You, Pam and Pete."

One block up from the shuttered gift shop is a small shopping center that is anchored by a small family-owned restaurant and a chain retailer.

Sandwiched between these are smaller spaces that have unfortunately been recently turned over. Among the casualties are a dress shop, a vitamin shop, and a bookstore.

How many jobs were lost? No one knows.

Does anybody care?

Every job lost creates a void.

Local communities receive a distribution of the state sales tax; for every closure, the community loses that income. The state of California loses the taxes paid by those employees, as well as the portion paid by the business.

For those of you thinking of starting a business, you'll be rudely shocked by the taxes the government puts on the employers.

Employers must match all Social Security, Medicare, and other contributions paid by the employees. Yeah, that's eyes-glazing-over stuff.

Let me state it another way. Call it a thirty percent surcharge tax every time you hire someone! You hire someone for $10 an hour and wham, you get taxed $3 an hour.

And that's off the top. When you are successful and turn a profit, government will take another round of cash from you.

Unless of course you are GE! Main Street can't park its profits offshore. Who thought it fair to exempt GE from taxes, but not Main Street—the largest creator of new jobs?

Ahhh, but this is an apolitical book. We're not even going to get into that discussion. We're not going to ask the question why GE president Jeffrey Immelt is Obama's job czar. This is the man who fired 20% of his US workforce—34,000 American jobs—to outsource them throughout the world.

I guess someone has to look out for GE's profits over there.

The federal, state, and local governments should be grateful to you, the small business owner, for creating jobs. But no, you get taxed the same as if you are filling your car's tank with gas and driving on public roads. That makes sense. Taxes pay for the roads.

But why would government tax the entrepreneur who creates jobs? To cover public employee pensions?

Well, it's because the government *can*. Mom-and-pop don't lobby the politicians. Labor does. Big business does. GE does.

Going deeper, this represents additional income to the employees that the employee doesn't see. A hidden tax.

I don't care what side of the political aisle you are on, but please, don't give me anymore stats about how many people don't pay taxes. Everyone who has a job and everyone who buys something from a store or who buys a gallon of gas pays taxes.

When you continue up Main Street there is another strip center. This one has three empty storefronts.

There's a gym that if you peeked through the windows you'd be able to see the mail stacked against the door—another graveyard of lost jobs. There's a vacant real estate office. With the crash of the real estate market, many real estate brokers and employees have lost their jobs.

Next door to the vacant real estate office was the hair salon my wife used to patronize.

Unfortunately, due to a lack of cash flow and the realization the hours she was working weren't yielding nearly the return needed, the owner closed her doors. At the time she closed, she had been employing four people.

Consider the ripple effect of this one store closing: four people lost their jobs, the city lost revenues from sales tax, the state of California lost their share of income tax, and the federal government lost its share of the pie.

With the closing, the usage of water, electricity, and gas were all eliminated. Those utilities lost revenue and profits, and reduced their tax payments.

The trickle-down effect of that one salon's closure impacts hundreds of vendors and small manufacturers of hair supplies as well.

Think of the number of products in a beauty shop and the hundreds of hair product suppliers that sell to mom-and-pop shops like this one; they lose their income on all of these products, reducing their taxes.

The rippling effect from these closings has a negative impact on our economy and expands exponentially.

In this section of La Cañada, approximately twenty percent of the retail space is vacant; all of it is space that isn't producing revenue for the city, county, state, or nation.

Check the demographics. La Cañada is one of the more influential areas in the country. Its public schools consistently rate at the top. But it wasn't immune to the economic disaster. No one was.

The crisis on Main Street is stark when you start to add up all of the businesses that have been closed, one community at a time.

There is one fast-food place still open. A Subway sandwich shop.

Subways aren't company owned. They are owned by small business owners. Franchisees.

In 2007, it was safe to assume if you owned a Subway sandwich franchise it was worth three times its annual sales revenues. Today, if you tried to sell a Subway store at three times revenues you would be carefully questioned as to the state of your mental acuity.

By 2011, the valuations of Subway stores had dropped to two times revenue.

It is a simple matter of supply and demand. The decreased amount of credit for Main Street makes credit not only expensive but inaccessible. The credit market has shrunk dramatically, and thus the demand for purchasing Subway units has decreased along with revenue.

Almost all Main Street businesses have experienced a decline to their business valuations.

Why is this important? Lower business valuations translate to less collateral, which translates to less capital for Main Street.

Everyone on Main Street has been hit—not only those businesses that closed but the ones who have managed to survive.

Chapter 2: Where We Are Today

One of my favorite shows is the History Channel's "Pawn Stars."

It's a family-owned small business—three generations are involved: Rick, the middle-aged, bald guy; his son Cory; and his dad, "the Old Man."

The show doesn't deal with the destitute who are down on their luck and need to pawn a wedding ring. Rather, it shows the glamorous, unique items people want to sell— Rembrandt paintings, Shelby Mustangs, Civil War guns.

For both lenders and borrowers, if there's an analogy for how small business lending looks in 2011, it's this show.

The Pawn Stars are lenders. Pawning was the earliest form of lending.

Watching the Pawn Stars ply their trade helps bankers understand the "new think." Well, it's not really new, it's old school, and that's the point.

The world of small business lending has changed, and it's back to the basics. Back to Credit 101. Back to the day.

In my day, I was a long-haired, wet-behind-the-ears junior small-business lending officer for Security Pacific Bank (now part of Bank of America) in Los Angeles's hot, smoggy, late-1970's San Fernando Valley.

The world was a little different.

Our bosses smoked at their desks and drank several double scotches at lunch—especially the female vice presidents.

The younger generation kept it more low-key, usually ordering two white wines at client lunches. Today this behavior would make us alcoholics headed for rehab.

No one knew the term sexual harassment. Diversity was just being introduced. We never dreamed of using computers—that was something for NASA. Don't ask, don't tell was mandatory for the gay crowd if they wanted to keep their jobs. Oh, we gossiped, but no one was out of the closet. That was reserved for some of our special Hollywood clients.

At twenty-five, I thought I was a big shot because I had my own assistant.

Air-conditioned cars were a luxury. Obesity was a sign of power. Hamburgers and beer were common fare for lunch for the younger bankers when we were not with the bosses or customers.

Don't get me wrong—I don't long for the days of yore. The prime rate hit 22%. Unemployment was rampant. Good luck buying gas.

Remember the odd/even license plate system where you could only buy gas on even or odd days depending on the last digit of your license plate?

There was no credit desert; it was a credit *void*. Credit, like gas, was gone.

The Iranian hostage crisis hung like a swinging blade ready to fall on our heads.

Russia invaded Afghanistan. Jimmy Carter invaded Iran with eight helicopters. That didn't work out so well.

The Russians had the bomb and their leaders let us know they would use it, constantly reminding us of our tenuous hold on life.

The nuclear freeze activists demanded "No Nukes." They grew up to become today's green activists, conveniently forgetting about another freeze they were screaming about due to oil consumption—the coming ice age.

But that didn't matter. We would be out of oil by the year 2000.

Hal Lindsey wrote *The Late Great Planet Earth*, a book implying Armageddon was coming soon.

Hell, I clearly remember watching our president blame *me* for our country's malaise.

At this time, the bank paid for my MBA at the University of Southern California and there I learned the five C's of credit: character, collateral, cash flow, capacity, and conditions.

It was a bank officer's Holy Grail. "Make sure every credit has the five C's," we were told, along with the corresponding mantra: "No one has ever been fired for turning down a loan."

One of the reasons for the popularity of the Pawn Stars lies in the fact there are numerous practical takeaways.

You could write a separate book about that.

In fact Pawn Stars is a classic small-business case study: running a family business, family succession issues, culture, work place standards, branding, core business values, managing millennia kids, cash flow management, gross profit margin management, inventory management, appropriate levels of risk, inventory acquisition, credit underwriting standards—there's a treasure trove of great stuff for entrepreneurs and bankers to learn from.

The Old Man

In the "Pawn Stars," the Old Man is the quintessential old-timer caricature: stuck in his ways and always reminiscing about how things were "back in the day"—not necessarily better or worse, it just was what it was.

The ownership of the business is split between the Old Man and his son Rick, with the Old Man owning 49% and Rick owning 51%. But watchers of the show quickly understand it is the Old Man who steers the course of the business with a firm hand.

Those who fail to heed the direction of the Old Man do so at their own peril. This is a fact of life; everyone has to answer to an Old Man.

Bankers, more than others, have multiple layers of "Old Mans" they must satisfy.

Start with the regulators. The overseers. Bankers have multiple layers of regulations, telling them how their business should be run. These guys enforce the rules.

Which makes sense. We don't want a repeat of the Great Depression where a bank failure would wipe out a family's nest egg.

If people entrust you with their money, there needs to be high standards to ensure that the money is safe.

The problem is that the regulators must strike the appropriate balance between protecting depositor money, and allowing credit to flow to Main Street. But I'm getting ahead of myself.

Bankers have many "Old Mans" to satisfy.

The Pawn Stars' Old Man is very clear on how he wants the business run, what type of loans he wants to make, and the valuation of collateral.

He runs a tight ship (yes, the pun is intended based on his naval background). Don't let his goofy antics fool you; he has a clear understanding of profit margins and overhead.

Trust me when I say that when they cut to shots of him counting money, that is not a "make-do" job. He understands his business is lending and cash is the asset that he uses to generate profit.

The items lining his shop are simply the last step in converting cash and using cash to generate profit.

To understand the concept of the Old Man, you have to understand the culture of a bank. It is a little-known secret that most bankers wield minimal power.

Loans are made through a committee. Employees must be hired through a human resources department. Purchases must be approved. Don't even try to expense alcohol anymore. One banker I know can't get reimbursed for restaurant tips greater than ten percent.

This hammer of authority builds layers upon layers of Old Men who must be satisfied. There is the loan committee, the audit committee, the board of directors, and of course the boss. Outside Old Men are numerous: auditors, accountants, lawyers, state regulators, and federal regulators.

A number of my client bankers are Small Business Administration (SBA) lenders. That adds more layers of scrutiny.

Why am I telling you this?

Because for the small business borrower, ultimately, these are the faceless Old Men (and nowadays many Old Women, but for convenience we'll stick with one designation) who directly impact your ability to get a loan.

SBA lenders must satisfy several departments at the SBA. These Old Men are very intrusive in the operations in the daily life of the bankers.

Take the Office of the Comptroller of Currency (OCC). Their job is reviewing the safety and soundness of a bank's loan.

The greatest concern the OCC has is that the bank is using poor judgment when it comes to evaluating the financial health of their potential borrowers.

A character quirk that makes an entrepreneur successful can be cast in a completely different light by the cold, analytical, steely view of the outside bankers.

Global cash flow is the buzzword at the moment.

Auditors are not only concerned with the operation of the small business, but also how the owners of the company respect their own personal cash and how they treat it as an asset.

Business owners who view their companies as personal ATMs to support a extravagant lifestyle are put on watch lists.

The regulators want to know if the loan is truly for investing in the company's assets (to purchase inventory, hire labor, pay overhead) or if the loan is used to support a lifestyle.

Yachts, planes, and villas in Rome can be the fruits of a successful entrepreneur; however, regulators loathe financing these toys because it screams a terrible lack of values and good judgment—at least to bureaucrats making $80,000 a year.

When viewed by a technocrat working as a GS 12 for the government in a cubicle out of Cleveland, their definition of "extravagant" will be different than the celebrity chef running a restaurant in Beverly Hills.

Or the small business owner in Peoria.

If you walk into the bank, proud of that fact that you own your family's vacation property on a secluded Minnesota lake, don't be shocked, and be prepared to answer, when your Old Man, the banker, asks why you don't sell that property and use the cash for your business.

And remember, it is not just the banker whom you must schmooze; you also must provide the answers for all of the other Old Men that they report to.

Today, banks are starting to lend to Main Street.

But slowly.

There are those businesses that have made it; that have survived.

My Quest for Answers

Before I began to write this book, I wanted to know what separated the winners from the losers. I got in the car and talked to small business owners. All over the country, whenever I got off a plane I sought out Main Street.

I wanted to find the answer to the question of supply versus demand.

Is it because banks refuse to lend money? They don't have a supply of money? Or is it demand? Is small business simply hunkering down to weather the storm and has become risk averse?

Why is lending starved on Main Street?

Bankers I have talked to are fairly uniform in their response. It's a demand issue, I'm told. Not enough quality applications are walking through the door.

Small business has a different view. The number-one concern for small business owners is accessibility to credit.

But they're not brooding over it. They're moving on and making their business recession-proof. Without their banker's help.

I also wanted to know how small businesses survived. What made them special? How were they different than those next door to them, or down the block?

My printer, Erik Ovanespour in La Cañada, opened up his shop eight years ago. He started as a photography development lab. When digital photography exploded he had to diversify, or he would have been another Main Street casualty.

His secret for survival?

He's added new business lines—studio photography, graphic design, Christmas cards, banners—anything that would make him relevant to his customers.

He's stayed ahead of the technological curve. He'll lease new machines to offer his customers the latest shiny experience.

"I need to be able to give my customers the product they need. It takes a lot of effort and a lot of energy to get someone to not only walk through the door the first time, but to get them to come back time and again. I need to be able to take care of them."

What can be more competitive than operating a dry cleaning store? They're all over the place.

Andreh Nazarian of Nu-Way Cleaning knows how to differentiate his store from the others. He, his wife, and his cousin *memorize* your name and phone number. That's how your order is stored.

If he sees you coming from the parking lot he's already punching your phone number into his computer to get your clothes before you even set foot into the store.

My dentist picked last year to expand. He was one of the few who got new financing last year. Dr. Marias of Burbank said his office makeover was worth it.

"I wanted everything neat and clean. That's what they see now coming through the office. For me, it was a good time to expand the business."

One of the more entertaining visits I made was to Game Equipment in the swamps of Louisiana. Two hours out of New Orleans. In August.

Talk about being in the middle of nowhere.

Their CEO, David Chadwick, told me they had to adapt and open up new markets to survive. He manufactures tractors and wagons and ships them to third-world countries.

While a lot of manufacturers were closing their doors he not only survived, with the help of a small business loan he expanded his plant and hired new employees.

Now, I'm a smart person. I have an MBA from the University of Southern California. I learned if you didn't make profits you would go out of business.

Poor marketing decisions wouldn't help. Organization of systems was critical. Planning was key. I learned the importance of market studies and business plans.

I still don't know why I had to take Quantitative Analysis and figure out the answer of what time will a plane arrive in Los Angeles if it took off from Cleveland at noon and flew at 500 mph with a head wind of 30 mph. I actually got all the calculations right, but I forgot about the time zones!

Or that if you have four tellers, and Teller A takes an average of 30 seconds to complete a transaction, Teller B takes 45 seconds, Teller C takes 27 seconds, and Teller D takes one minute, and you were the fifth person in line, what is the standard deviation of how long you will have to wait in line? Remember, this was before ATMs. Everyone waited in line. Well, that was easy; I worked in a bank, so I didn't have to wait in line!

But, I didn't really understand the dynamics of small business survival.

Small businesses don't fail because they don't make enough money, or they don't have money in the bank, or their bank canceled their credit card account, or the bookkeeper stole a couple of thousand dollars.

Don't get me wrong—any of these events can be devastating.

But simply, the reason why most small businesses fail is the entrepreneur just gives up.

It becomes too hard.

A small business can survive negative cash flow, lawsuits, regulatory burdens, the harassing collection calls, the power being turned off. As long as the owner shows up, they'll figure it out.

But once the drive is gone, once the feeling of helplessness takes root, it's all over. The fight is simply too tough.

Today, the banker wants the answer to one simple question: Will you do what it takes to keep the business open and pay back your loan?

Don't be like Ted Kennedy who flubbed the question in 1976 on why he wanted to be president. He didn't have an answer.

If you can't answer the simple question of why you want to do this, just keep walking down the road and don't even bother to walk through the banker's door.

Chapter 3: What Happened to the Small Business Lenders?

How does a bank make money?

A bank is a business no different than any Main Street retailer; they buy low and sell high. What are they selling? A product that they make.

For example, take any Main Street restaurant.

That restaurant will buy food from the local farmers market and truck it to their shop. The cook will take the raw materials and create a meal that comes out of the kitchen doors and is presented to the customer via a waiter or waitress.

A bank takes its raw material—money—and hires a credit officer to consider your circumstances, match it to the money, and create the bank's product—a loan.

How does a bank buy low and sell high?

The bank has access to capital at extremely low interest rates. Banks can borrow money from the federal government at less than one percent interest.

In turn, they loan it out to their best customers at five percent interest.

For every $100,000 in loans, that's a $4,000 profit each year.

And they're not like the Pawn Stars where they have to negotiate the price and get stuff low.

They simply walk up to the fed's money window and help themselves. Now that's a nice model.

And it scales from there. The higher the risk, the more they charge. It's tough being a bank apologist when they charge 29% for credit card debt.

I'll committee that discussion for another day.

It's an interesting business model, treating cash as inventory. A normal business (and yes I concede that perhaps a bank is abnormal in its business practices) wants to conserve cash.

In fact, one of the biggest takeaways from the Great Recession and one of the common themes of business, be it Main Street, Middle Market, or Fortune 500, is that business people want to conserve cash. They want to have access to cash, they want to have cash in the bank, and they want to have cash readily available.

The lesson for the survivors of the recession has been clear: cash was a needed commodity not only to survive the Great Recession, but the threat of a "double dip."

This book doesn't discuss the economics of what will happen in the future.

We're simply presenting the fact that the majority of small business owners believe there will be an extension of the current difficult times. The only thing they know is that if they have cash in the bank, they can weather any storm.

But the bank is a business, and bankers are treating their businesses with the same cash concerns as any other.

To be fair though, the driving force on banks retaining their cash, which is their capital, are the regulators.

Consider this analogy to understand clearly the problems facing banks today.

Let's say that you own an Ace Hardware store and have thousands of items you are able to sell to your customers.

You can buy a common widget from your supplier for $2.50, and being a prudent businessperson, you mark it up 30% and sell it for $3.25. The customer comes into the store, a transaction is completed, and you've made a seventy-five cent profit.

Your ability to replicate this transaction through a number of different products allows you to put cash in the bank, which translates to electricity for the lights and payroll to pay your employees, as well as the taxes on your profit.

When the bank creates a $100,000 loan product, combining cash with a loan officer, analysis and approval, that is not a simple over-the-counter sale.

Don't worry, this isn't an accounting book that will glaze your eyes over, but everyone needs to understand this transaction has to be accounted for. There are a host of entities that tell the banker how to manage the transaction, notably the CPA and the regulators, which is where it gets interesting for the banker.

The Ace Hardware storeowner clearly understands what his or her profit is on any given item. They understand gross profit margin and they understand the transaction.

For the bank, it is not as simple as putting that $100,000 on their books and sitting back to create their profit. The bank has created a $100,000 product, and now their inventory needs to be accounted. The bank will charge a loan fee, which it can take into income right off the top, but the issue the bank must deal with is a concept called "Mark-to-Market Accounting."

Let me give you a simple analogy. You own a home that you purchased in 1999 for $150,000. In 2007, your neighbor buys the identical tract house for $300,000. A fair assumption at that point is that *both* houses are now worth $300,000.

At the height of the real estate boom in 2008, the neighbor on your other side sold his house for $500,000. All three houses are identical, thus the fair assumption is all three of the houses are worth $500,000, leaving you feeling pretty good about life and your situation.

Unfortunately, events you can't control now come into play. Your new neighbor refinances his house for $300,000.

You, being a prudent homeowner, have not refinanced your house and now only owe $100,000 on it. But in 2009, your neighbor is hit with a double whammy. The adjustable rate mortgage (ARM) he entered into doubles his payments and soon after he loses his job.

He tries to sell the house for what he owes on it, $300,000, but there are no takers. The foreclosure process goes through its normal channels and ends with the house being acquired by the bank, which in turn sells it for $250,000.

Following real estate industry practices, the value of *your* house is now $250,000.

And if you had followed the example of your neighbor and refinanced your now-valued-at-$250,000 house for $300,000, or bought the house at the height of market valuations for $500,000—well, you would be part of the 20% of the country who are in the same mess.

This is the problem the bankers face when they make a loan—the loan price has to be based upon "fair market value."

It's easy to equate this problem with commercial real estate, and that's why many are predicting a commercial real estate bubble collapse in 2011 and 2012. More on that later.

But the regulators don't stop with commercial real estate. They are looking at all loans.

If a bank makes a loan to a restaurant, the regulators will come and say to you, "Hey, twenty percent of all restaurant loans made since 2000 in SBA's lending programs have failed. Last year, five percent of all restaurants closed their doors. Therefore, we have to assume there is a five percent chance that this loan will fail. We need you to allocate a portion of the loan immediately to your 'loan loss reserve.'"

The loan loss reserve is an accounting mechanism that attempts to place fair market value on the bank's loans.

The problem is, if the regulators think there is a ten percent chance a loan will fail, certainly a fair assumption based on market statistics and the economic outlook, then the bank will have to immediately take a $10,000 write-off on that loan, putting it into a loss position.

If an Ace Hardware manufacturer were forced to sell the widget he acquired at $2.50 for $1.50, it is the same as if the Ace hardware retailer sold that plumbing unit for $1.50. It may be beneficial for quick cash, but the long-term sustainability for that model is unworkable.

Therefore, banks are reluctant to make loans when they have to incur an immediate write-off on the loan.

These are just some of the problems you will face when you walk through the door with your loan application. You will be eyed with open skepticism about whether your concept is going to work and what the bank will have to write off when they make the loan.

Who Are the Bankers?

Banking as a business has the same model as any other business.

Using the Madison Avenue advertising model, the banks have accounts people, who hold the client's hand and assure them throughout the process; and people who are the sales effort, charged with bringing new clients through the door.

The creative directors at these advertising agencies generate the product, but never work to close the deal. No different from the banks' chief credit officers.

It is extremely important that you understand where in the hierarchy the person you are dealing with resides.

Are you dealing with a salesperson, the accounts man, or the talent, the chief credit officer?

Or if things go bad, an asset recovery person? Don't be fooled by the name.

They aren't there to help *you* recover your assets.

Just as there are varying job descriptions for the generic "vice president" title, it is critical you clearly understand which of these people you are working with and how each impacts you differently.

While it is important to understand the actual hierarchical position of the person you are dealing with, you should also be mindful of the other bankers who will be touching your banking relationship that you will never meet.

I recently attended a small business banking conference in Texas. Approximately three hundred lenders met to discuss their products, which is essentially the inventory they're selling to small business bankers.

The head of Citigroup's small business lending unit, Raj Seshadri, said her greatest challenge is recruiting small business lenders who can adequately convey the bank's inventory (the bank's product) to small business owners.

Today, these positions are being filled by millennials—the generation of recent college graduates entering the business world. Odds are, your first contact with a bank to discuss a lending relationship will be with this class.

I use the word "class" on purpose; class indicates that there are a number of attributes to a specific group of people.

Don't worry, you don't need to know all of the statistics of how millennials operate (heavy use of technology, an indifferent view of religion, a penchant for delaying the rites of passage to adulthood, etc.), other than to know that these individuals do not have the life business experience that the chief credit officer of the bank will have.

This is not a negative statement, rather an "it is what it is" statement.

Contrast the millennial's business experience with that of the bank's current chief credit officer.

The chief credit officer of a bank will be a grey-haired, balding, overweight male or female, with no personality as a result of what they've gone through the past couple of years. They're lucky to have a job and know a lot of people who don't.

Look back at the timeline that these sixty-year-old professionals have encountered.

They started in banking in the late sixties or early seventies when inflation was rampant, running double digits, and was a truly insidious threat to the economy.

Inflation is an abstract concept that the millennials have never personally experienced. Their familiarity with the word correlates to whatever they've read in their economics or history books.

In the 1970s the young, up-and-coming chief credit officers who held the entry-level positions charged with talking to small business bankers personally suffered from the truly horrific economic downturn of the period. The prime rate hit 22%.

Not only did Main Street not have access to capital, there was *no* access to capital.

The entire United States banking system, as well as the world's, was in a complete economic freeze. The election of Ronald Reagan, depending on your point of view, greatly aided or hindered the economy in the eighties.

But, the S&L crisis closed 25% of savings and loans and cost the taxpayer $100 billion in bad real estate loans in the 1980s.

Our chief credit officers, now in their thirties, started to see an economic recovery. But in the late eighties a recession that some today would call a "double dip" brought the message back home: there will always be cycles of economic prosperity and bust. After another recession in the early nineties (remember Clinton's campaign slogan "It's the economy, stupid?") the country entered into a period of relative prosperity compared to other periods.

Stability continued until the next major factor hit the American economy, the dot-com bubble. Billions of dollars of overvalued tech stocks were eliminated and a tremendous number of people suffered financially.

That brings us to the present day, and we don't have to describe the results of the Great Recession.

The reason for the history lesson is you need to understand that the chief credit officer, who sets the loan policies and determines your loan's approval, has seen it all. They've seen wars, severe economic downturns, 500-year floods on the Mississippi, pestilence, and everything else but the locusts.

While the bank's chief credit officers may be up all night worried about the future, small business owners are definitely staying up at night worrying about the present.

I don't mean to paint a bleak picture; obviously, loans are being approved and funded in today's economy. This requires the mitigation of risk. One of the tools lenders use to mitigate their risk is to share it with the government with the SBA lending program.

The Small Business Administration

Now, you've probably guessed that I'm an SBA apologist.

The good news is I'm not going to load you up with a ton of facts.

I only need one argument to convince you of the worth of SBA's lending programs to Main Street:

The SBA didn't receive a bailout.

It seems like everyone else did. Check out of the list of who the taxpayers have bailed out during the Great Recession.

1) Freddie Mac
2) Fannie Mae
3) General Motors
4) Chrysler
5) AIG
6) General Electric
7) Bank of America
8) Citigroup
9) Wells Fargo
10) and hundreds of other banks

SBA is missing from the list. SBA didn't need a bailout. The program pays for itself from borrower and lender fees.

How it works is simple. The bank loans a small business the money. The federal government issues a piece of paper agreeing to guarantee a percentage of any loan losses, usually 75%, on a prorated basis with the lender.

The lender does all the work, approving, documenting, servicing, and if need be, liquidating the loan.

SBA 7(a) loans can be as small as $5,000 and as large as $5 million. Main Street can use the loans for general working capital or purchasing commercial real estate.

One of the most advantageous features of the SBA loan for the borrower is the term of the loan. Because of the government guaranty, lenders can term the loan out for ten years for working capital purposes, and 25 years for real estate. That's a fully amortized loan, with no prepayment penalty and no balloon payment.

The risk to the federal government is small, even with outstanding guaranties of over $50 billion.

In 2011, small business bankers will lend $17 billion worth of 7(a) loans to Main Street.

A journalist once actually asked me what would happen if the federal government had to write a check for all its outstanding SBA guaranties.

"Well," I said, "We just got through an economic meltdown giving $787 billion to Wall Street. Main Street didn't need to call its measly $50 billion guaranties; those were still good. But if we ever get to the point where all those small businesses default, we'll be in the middle of a total economic collapse and that discussion will be moot."

The other major program is SBA's 504 lending program. It's designed for businesses that need to expand by acquiring new property and equipment, thus creating jobs.

Under this program, the lender makes a first lien position loan of 50% of the purchase price, trust deed, or mortgage, depending on your state. That loan can be up to $5.5 million.

An intermediary—a certified development company—will arrange a second lien loan of 40%. That loan is sold to Wall Street and guaranteed by the federal government.

Kurt Chilcott runs the nation's largest SBA 504 lender, CDC Small Business Lending out of San Diego, loaning over $300 million a year. SBA 504 lending will top $4 billion this year.

In 2010, SBA 7(a) lending was up 34%. Though statistics can be twisted, the optimist would point to that 34% figure as a positive. The pessimist though, would ask you to consider how that percentage was arrived at since 2009 was the low point of SBA lending.

2005 was the peak of SBA lending. At that time, CIT Small Business Lending led all SBA 7(a) lenders in volume, holding the top spot from 2000-2008. In 2005, their total loan volume was $800 million.

Bank of America was the top SBA 7(a) lender in number of loans from 2002-2007. By the end of 2005, they had 12,000 loans, continuing a streak of being over ten thousand loans each year from 2004 to 2007.

In 2009, as lending fell dramatically off the cliff, the lending industry was in the spiral of a death dance.

In 2010, the top lender in terms of numbers was JP Morgan Chase with just over 3,000 loans—a drastic change from the peak of 2005. Bank of America is not even on the chart. CIT went through a "restructure," it went bankrupt, and is a shadow of its former self in the SBA lending world.

Recognizing the cost effectiveness of small business lending, Congress and the Administration offered various "stimulus" provisions that have increased SBA lending.

They have worked. While still not close to the peak of five years ago, there are loans being funded.

Let's take a look at the SBA lending industry—and yes, it is an industry. The successful small business borrower must understand the dramatic changes that have occurred in SBA lending.

For example, Coleman Publishing has 10,000 email subscribers to our daily reports. The majority of the subscribers are small business bankers. To illustrate how much the lending industry has been disrupted, between 2008 and 2009 twenty-five percent of our email subscribers lost their jobs. Now those jobs are coming back, but at a cost.

While we've talked about the paunchy, graying, chief credit officers, those positions have remained relatively unchanged.

The change has come on the street, from the accounts person, the sales person, or whoever the small business borrower interacts with initially when they try to get their loan.

No one will admit it, but a large swath of experienced, older, highly paid sales people have exited the industry and they're not coming back.

The banks won't admit it, but they've replaced these highly paid, highly skilled professionals with a new generation of lender. No banker would confess to this wholesale change, mainly because they don't want to open themselves up to an age discrimination lawsuit.

The reality is that these changes have occurred and have forever altered the way banks manage their small-business lending portfolios.

And taking the other side of the coin, perhaps this is not a bad shift. Remember, this was the group of "lending professionals" that saw one in five of their SBA loans default.

Think about that number: for every failed loan, there is a litany of lost jobs, broken dreams, lost tax revenues and in general just the residue of a septic tank.

No good story can come from those statistics. Banks had to change the way they did business. Let's turn back the clock to 2005 (the peak of small business lending), look at the top small business lenders, and see where they are today.

Bank of America

Bank of America was the largest SBA 7(a) lender in 2005. Despite the recent press of Bank of America building up its small-business lending department, they have fled from SBA 7(a) lending.

In 2008, Bank of America made a little over 3,000 SBA 7(a) loans for $100 million as part of their overall small-business lending portfolio.

But their overall losses mounted.

The attitude of Bank of America is best described by Ken Lewis in October 2008. Then the company's CEO, he infamously called the bank's small business loan portfolio a "damn disaster."

In 2010, the bank made only 185 SBA 7(a) loans for $20 million, ranking them 88th in the 2010 *Coleman Report 500*. It was a far cry from their position at the top five years earlier.

They claim their drop-off is due to a *demand shortage* and a *lack of qualified borrowers*.

Main Street would disagree

CIT Small Business Lending

Not to be confused with CITIgroup, the largest SBA lender by volume was CIT Group's small business lending. You've probably heard about CIT in the news.

After all CIT was one of the largest TARP failures, costing taxpayers nearly $2 billion when they went bankrupt.

They are a specialty financing company, and different from a bank in that they don't accept deposits.

The problem with CIT wasn't their small-business lending portfolio *per se*, but losses in some of the other ten or twelve business product lines that they offer, namely student loans.

The real problem that CIT encountered was a sustainability problem. After the commercial paper market crashed in 2008, they found out they could not finance their long-term, 25-year loans with 90-day commercial paper.

CIT is coming back. They don't have the numbers that they once did, but they are still a relevant lender.

Their small-business lending unit president, Chris Reilly, has survived, and like every other small-business lender who still has a job, she is much smarter than five years ago. Her words, not mine.

And if you think about it, small-business borrowers hardly gave the financial viability of their lending institution a second glance.

Today, a small-business owner can do business with many companies that fell bankrupt in 2009, including buying their car, writing a check to their landlord, and even borrowing money from a lender.

BLX and Others

Our classic tale of lender woes is the one about Business Loans Express.

BLX exceeded industry average with loan losses exceeding 30% of its portfolio and one of their executive vice presidents was sentenced to ten years in federal prison for loan fraud.

They were once the second-largest SBA lender.

Today they are bankrupt.

There are also a couple of other names on the list that no longer exist. The failure of Wachovia Bank, which was taken over by Wells Fargo, decimated thousands of people's 401k plans.

Wachovia went on a buying spree and acquired a large number of local, well-operating community banks.

These banks had been in town for generations, and more importantly, the stock had been handed down from generation to generation. Dividends from stock in banks founded by grandfathers and great grandfathers had created legacy wealth from generation to generation.

When Wachovia bought the local community bank, nest eggs were converted into Wachovia stock.

And when Wachovia went bankrupt and was acquired by Wells Fargo, generations of wealth evaporated overnight.

Six-figure trust fund incomes vanished.

In 2005, Wachovia was the number four SBA lender.

Temecula Valley Bank was ranked 15th that same year. Real estate development loans in California's inland empire doomed the bank, and the federal government took it over, losing millions of dollars to the taxpayer.

Comerica Bank exited the SBA lending program as well.

Half of the top lenders in 2005 do not participate in SBA's lending program in 2011.

They simply chose to exit the small-business lending arena due to the high rate of losses. And we're not just talking about SBA loans, we're talking about small business in general.

Don't forget Washington Mutual. Another bankrupt lender. Add Indy-Mac to the list.

And of course, 150 other community banks that have faded from the scene with another 700 banks on the Fed's endangered species list.

Then there is Advanta. Once it was a sleepy, non-bank lender that made credit cards available to teachers. In the go-go days of the early 2000's, the company changed courses and began to aggressively market itself to the small business community. In 2008, the company had $6 billion in credit card loans to small businesses.

That company filed bankruptcy in 2009.

Advanta alone contributed six percent of the $1 trillion in lost credit card lines in the United States.

These horror stories reinforce the concept that small business lending is difficult. It is expensive and if not managed properly will sink institutions.

If you look at the numbers, we have bemoaned the fact that 20% of all the small businesses that received an SBA loan since 2000 have failed.

But those numbers are much better when you consider 50% of the top lenders who made an SBA loan have failed. Small business—which is inherently volatile—has a better track record than the established lenders!

With whom you choose to have business is crucial. If the FDIC takes over your institution, it is more than a mild inconvenience of where you're going to get your checks printed.

If you have a credit line, the available money will obviously go away.

If you owe money, you will now be dealing with a new entity—one that bought your loan at a discount for, say, eighty cents on the dollar.

They only way your new lender will make their money back is to collect the loan as quickly as possible.

There will be no negotiation for extending terms. No negotiation for a new credit line. There will only be a discussion on how quickly you will pay them, and the considerable legal resources the company holding your debt will use against you if you don't pay up.

Not a very pleasant prospect in today's credit-starved environment.

If you are fortunate enough to have more than $250,000 in cash, you need to realize that in the event of a bank failure you could quickly become an unsecured creditor. And don't assume that if you have your money at CitiFinancial or Bank of America that all is well. The current political environment has made it clear that "Too Big to Fail" will not be the law of the land the next time around.

It is an easy prediction to say that we will have another Lehman Brothers-type failure with a large bank going into receivership at the next economic turndown.

A small business owner now must not only take the necessary steps to understand their own financial statements, but they must learn how to read a bank financial statement.

Chapter 4:

The New Bank Lending Model

I was tempted to title this book *What Small Business Owners and Bankers Need to Learn from the Pawn Stars.*

But, if you watch the show, you know how tough these guys are in negotiations. I figured by the time I cut a deal to use their name in the title they would own half the book and I would end up working graveyard for them on Saturday nights to boot.

But what can we learn from the Pawn Stars?

First, they are a small business. A family-owned business. And these guys are shrewd. And fair. At least on TV! (Remember it's the pig that ends up getting slaughtered.)

If I was a banker and hired a kid right out of college I wouldn't send them to banking school. I would buy a DVD of the show, put them in the conference room, lay in some deli sandwiches and just have them watch the show.

Most of what you need to know about small business lending can be learned from watching Pawn Stars.

Let's look at the Pawn Stars business model. How do they lend money?

When a customer enters their shop, the Pawn Stars don't run out and ask an appraiser what he or she thinks the customer's merchandise is worth. That number is immaterial to them.

That's about all you need to know in the change in bank-think over the past several years. Bankers and their regulators are no longer in love with what a third party—an appraiser—says something is worth.

That didn't work out so well for either the big insurer AIG or the local community bank in Greely, Colorado. No one relies on what an appraiser says something is worth.

They want to know what it can be *sold* for.

Take an uncirculated twenty-dollar St. Gauden's double-eagle gold coin.

After a quick check on the Internet, or a phone call to a coin dealer, you may think the coin is worth $2,000.

But those numbers mean absolutely nothing to the Pawn Stars.

The driving factor for the Pawn Stars in determining value is what someone is willing to pay for this item.

That is the only number that matters. They're not concerned about appraised value, only the value that moves the item off the shelf.

Our Pawn Stars have become experts in valuation, not a "paper" valuation, but what someone is willing to pay for the item *today.*

Bankers in the post-Great Recession will do the same thing. They know their community.

Community bankers know their towns, and which properties can sustain a Main Street business and those that can't for whatever reason.

If you ask any competent community banker about the history of a specific location, she may say that in the past ten years, seven businesses have been in that location and you would be the eighth. And since the odds are that in two years there will be a ninth, you won't be receiving any financing.

If you are on a Main Street with a history of stable businesses, you will have a greater chance of obtaining financing to open a location in that area.

Bankers want to know, and have learned that they need to know, who is going to take them out of the deal.

They don't want a piece of paper that says this commercial real estate is worth $500,000. They can take that piece of paper and throw it away, as it is essentially worthless in today's environment.

After all, that's what the bank regulators do!

They want to know: Who in the community has the resources or has the ability to take them out of the deal in a worst-case scenario?

When you are sitting down with your banker to explore financing possibilities, it would be prudent for you to explain to that banker how they are going to be able to extricate themselves from a poor position.

In the old days, this is what would be called a cosigner. A young kid would go in to buy a car, and the banker would shake their head gravely, and then mom or dad, or Uncle Harry, would have to come in and sign. The banker knew that if the kid didn't pay his loan, family would.

Commercial transactions are a little more complicated, but the same premise holds true.

If you come in with a piece of paper that says something is worth $500,000, the banker will obviously smile warmly at your good fortune, but you will still have to convince him or her of what happens when something goes wrong.

Most people don't have that knowledge base, but your banker does. The banker is already starting to scroll through in his or her head the players in the community who could be potential investors and who would be interested in this property at a substantial discount.

That is a huge thought process shift from 2005.

A common criticism of bankers is that they are not businessmen. They're viewed as technocrats sitting on their vault of cash in a large corporate environment, above the fray of running a business and free of cash flow problems.

This perception, however, is flat-out wrong and those who ignore that fact do so at their own peril.

Bankers are sophisticated businessmen, and in fact most bankers work for a small business and in a small office environment: the community bank.

While a banker may not have the same pressures of needing cash in the bank to make payroll or paying bills, they certainly have the same pressures in terms of profit and loss.

Everyone knows that profit and cash flow is how Main Street derives its revenues. The bank is no different.

If someone walks into a Main Street store and purchases their product, the proceeds go directly to that small business. The bank, which also has a storefront on Main Street, uses the same business model.

People walk into their store, purchase a product, and the bank receives proceeds. The bank's product happens to be cash. There are other services as well including payroll service, credit card processing, and ATM fees, but the bank's primary source of revenue is in the form of loans.

A bank simply cannot be profitable without lending out cash.

Loans are the banks' inventory, no different from a flower shop's flowers or a baker's bread.

However, similar to the flower shop owner whose inventory can wilt, or the baker's product that can go stale, the banker has a similar problem in that if the borrower doesn't pay back the loan, the bank's inventory is wasted and will cause a loss.

This is the tricky part of banking and why they are so meticulous. Heck, just call it anal.

It is a strange concept.

Main Street makes money by selling its product or its service. Once the cash is collected the transaction is completed.

Banks make money by lending money out, collecting upfront fees, and collecting interest. But the base is only as strong as the borrowers' collective ability to make payments on their loans, and the anticipated revenue stream from those payments.

The current credit crisis is the perfect example of what can happen when the bank's inventory goes sour. Unlike the widget manufacturer, whose inventory of different electrical products is stored in a huge warehouse serviced by an army of forklift drivers, a bank's inventory is simply lifted from a computer printout.

The value of their inventory is only as good as the people who have signed their names on the loans. If the people who've signed their names stop making their loan payments, then the bank's assets are worthless.

We are not going to rehash the history of what happened. There are much better books about that, but a number of major institutions were taken down during the subprime crisis.

The landscape is littered with former Wachovias, Washington Mutuals, and hundreds of community bank branches, all of which failed simply because someone showed that the numbers on the computer printouts were overinflated and had no underlying value.

That happened to a top-ten SBA small business lender, Temecula Valley Bank in Southern California, not because of SBA, but because of its real estate lending practices.

What this means for today's business borrowers is that they must do everything to convince the small-business banker that their loan will be paid come hell or high water.

In 2007, when credit was flowing like rain, an applicant could walk into a bank, show they had a couple hundred thousand dollars of equity in their house, and be running a Quiznos' Sub Shop in thirty days.

Those days are long gone; and while it is imprudent to say never, it will certainly be a long time before we return to the credit standards of 2007.

What does the small business borrower face today? When you sit across the desk from the banker, the banker is evaluating the totality of your application.

Don't confuse business planning with a business plan. Planning is essential.

Business Plans

I get very frustrated when talking to supposed small-business loan experts or when I read guides on how to start a small business and the first words that pop up on the page are that you must prepare a business plan.

Business plans are great if you are taking on extra capital and are convincing a venture capital lender to put their money in a concept or technology that is difficult to explain in concise terms.

They say business plans are needed to create a road map from concept to cash revenue.

But the secret of a successful entrepreneur is adaptability. I don't know one entrepreneur who wrote a business plan that hit the numbers one or two years out.

You might as well spend your time trying to write the next great vampire novel.

Outstanding concepts, such as Twitter, are amazingly effective in capturing a new market.

But even Twitter wrestles with the problem of figuring out how to monetize their business model today. They certainly had ideas when they started out, but their "plan" was to get people to use it and then work out the numbers later.

A business plan is essentially no help for the person trying to open a Main Street sandwich shop. Detailing the demographics in one, three, and five-mile concentric circles continues to be a tree killer.

The only thing that matters is if you can get people to give you cash for your product.

Presenting the banker a twenty-five-page thesis that would have earned you an "A" in college does nothing to advance the cause of getting that banker all warm and fuzzy about your business ideas.

The most difficult process that the small business borrowers don't understand is the banker wants to see *performance*.

Getting people to give you cash or write you a check is an extremely difficult proposition. Setting up a storefront operation and getting people to walk through that door and depart without their money is a daunting task.

This is why bankers run in the other direction when people present them with a start-up opportunity, be it a franchise or mom-and-pop operation.

What does the banker want to see? That the totality of your application will put you in the upper tier of their loan assets.

The community banker knows their Main Street, the businesses on it, the demographics, and the basics of a common business plan, all of which make it easier for him or her to evaluate whether you're a serious player or a dreamer.

Contrast that with the fresh-out-of-college, wet-behind-the-ears banker sitting in a cubicle in Phoenix, talking to someone in Tampa. He or she does not have the luxury of knowing the local environment.

If you want to convey the sense that you are a serious player, you will do a different type of assignment than any college professor would assign. The banker doesn't want to know how many one-and-one-half baths are in houses in a three-mile concentric circle.

They want to know what makes your concept special enough to get people to walk in the doors.

Let's use the example of the restaurant.

One of the great disconnects in the small business lending industry is the fact that we all see the failure rates for restaurants are staggering, yet restaurants continue to be the number one receiver of small business loans.

How can this happen?

Bankers aren't stupid and they know the risks that come with restaurants, but they still do it. If you want to be one of those restaurant small-business borrowers, you need to first convince yourself that the business is viable and then convince the Old Man sitting behind the desk.

Your homework assignment—your business plan—should include sitting on a corner with a clipboard counting cars entering a parking lot, accurately determining how many people eat in the area, every competitor's operation, and not only understanding their product but also having an understanding of their financial situation.

In fact, if you are really serious, go work at a competitor for six months. Who does that these days? Those who don't want to go bankrupt, that's who.

Also, you would be surprised of the wealth of information you can get by striking up a conversation with the owner.

Most will reveal a lot more about their operation than they should. I was in Alaska a couple years ago when a salmon-fish-fry restaurant owner detailed his entire business plan to me, including the gross profit margins from what the cruise ships paid him to feed their passengers lunch on the daily tour.

But you'd better be smart enough to separate the truth from fiction.

When I was a banker I worked for an Old Man who left USC in 1946 after one year and opened up a hot dog stand. A World War Two vet, he was—hmmm wrong adjective, *is*—still alive and kicking at ninety.
He was a bomber pilot but fortunately for him his assignment was ferrying B-29s between the Boeing factory in Seattle to Riverside March Air Force base for shake-out, and then to Pearl Harbor where they were ferried to the Far East for combat. He caught a ride to Seattle and repeated the process.

After the war, and USC, he decided he wanted to be the next great hot dog entrepreneur.

He was making a little money, but after a couple of months he had already soured on the idea and he and his partner decided to split up and sell the business.

He put out the word.

One potential buyer said, "Interesting business, how much money do you make?"

"Oh I don't know," the Old Man would say, "All I know is we pay cash for everything. Whatever is left in the till when we close, we split it up 50/50 and go home." And then with a wink he said, "But we're taking home a lot of money."

"Well, how much?" the potential buyer would ask.

Despite the prodding, the Old Man would still continue to say, "I don't know, but it's a lot."

Finally the Old Man said, "I'll tell you what, why don't you come by here tomorrow and watch how many people come by the stand. We'll count the money together at the end of the night when we close."

The intrigued prospect showed up the next day to find there was a line that stretched around the block. The area was overflowing. They checked the cash register at closing and sure enough there was a lot of money. A *lot* of money.

The buyer yelled, "This is a gold mine! How much do you want out of it?"

"Oh, I'm tired, the hours are long. I don't need a lot. I just want enough money so I can do something else," the Old Man said wryly.

A deal was quickly struck and the Old Man left hot dogs to begin to amass his fortune in furniture, and later banking.

What the buyer did not see was that the Old Man had been handing out dollar bills at the end of the line. He was buying everyone who happened by a free hot dog and drink.

No wonder the till was full of cash.

In 2011, you need to understand the market. You need to understand what is real and what is hot dogs. That's why business valuations are now a "must" for small business lenders.

A Small Business Banker Now Employs a Number of Experts

A cottage industry of experts has sprung up to give lenders expert advice.

The requirement for real estate property appraisals by real estate appraisers is obvious.

Any hint of an ancient Native American burial site? Of civil war dead? Studies must be conducted by more experts to ensure no remains exist.

Tennessee requires lenders get "historical waivers" to ensure new projects don't disturb places of historical significance.

Environment impact reports are a must for larger projects.

Another type of consultant is an engineering firm. These are critical outside experts that all lenders will employ. Changes in liability laws during the 1980s put lenders at risk if they foreclosed on a property where there was environmental damage.

As the new legal owner of that property, the lender is now responsible for any clean up. Whether it be a junkyard, underground fuel tanks, or pools of leftover chemicals, the lender has to know what its exposure is on that property and will hire an engineering firm to conduct a preliminary assessment if there is a potential exposure to the lender.

Don't be fooled by that corner lot on Main Street that's housing a building built in the 1970s. A lender will want to know if a gasoline station was there back in the 1950s.

If there was some type of underground tank on that property, the lender could be liable for removing the tank and digging up the contaminated dirt, a horribly expensive process. That is the reason financing gasoline stations is almost next to impossible today.

Another type of outside expert are those who validate the assets of a business.

Typically, these are accountants that will do an audit of a company's receivables and inventory. And don't be surprised if you are asked to go to your local college—not for you to attend classes, but to contact a group of students to help you with drafting a formal marketing plan.

I wrote earlier my disdain for formal business plans, but formal marketing plans can be a very useful exercise. Again, for demographic statistics, a marketing plan is very simple: identify the sources of entities (people and companies) who will write you a check for your product.

The old-school guys constantly search for knowledge to make sure they know what they have so they don't make bad decisions.

It took the Great Recession for today's bankers to embrace the same concept. Information mitigates bad decisions.

When something walks through the door that the Pawn Stars aren't familiar with, they don't hesitate to make a call to their roster of experts—Sean the gunsmith, the Clark County Museum curator, toy experts, coin experts, stamp experts, signature experts. They have a stable of people they trust for expert help.

And they don't mind ponying up to the table. The producers love to show the stories of people who find out their stuff is worth thousands, not just the hundreds they had hoped.

The Pawn Stars don't mind transparency. They know it's bad for business if they have a reputation of ripping people off. It's not a sustainable long-term strategy. They'll set the price, readily admit how much of a profit they expect to make, and try to cut a deal.

They have discovered it's easier to know exactly what they have in terms of authenticity and value than to guess.

In the past, small-business lenders guessed too much. The ease of which information can be obtained today at low cost helps lenders who want to stay in the game a long time, not just make a quick buck, and be around for the 2020 edition of this book.

The last outside expert is the cloud—the Internet. More on that later, but do some homework and Google yourself to prepare for a later chapter. Your banker already has.

Chapter 5:
The New Small Business Lenders

While change can be painful, new small business models for lending are developing.

How are loans getting done in today?

Here's one example.

Joe Wojtowicz is a loan broker out of Ohio. Two of his clients are Debra and Joe Lukaski, co-owners of two Subway franchises in Cleveland. They were looking to open a third at the Cleveland airport.

Several years ago Joe would have been able to go to one of the national lenders that would finance Subway concepts anywhere in the country.

That small business lending model has disappeared. There are no national franchise lenders in the marketplace today.

Instead of spending fruitless hours on the phone, Joe put the Lukaski's loan package on a new service called BoeFly, an online marketplace connecting borrowers with lenders.

They currently have 500 lenders signed up, and are adding more every day.

Joe told me nine banks from around the country wanted to take a look at the complete package.

And he found a community bank out of Colorado to fund the deal.

Sherwin Patidar of First Capital Bank would never have seen the deal if it weren't for BoeFly and the Internet.

The Lukaskis got their loan and created sixteen new jobs in the process.

Specialty lenders have emerged that make small business lending their niche.

Consider First Heritage Bank of Snohomish, Washington. Their president, Cathy Reines, knew quickly that the model they had of being a staid community bank lender was unsustainable. Ninety percent of their loan assets were in real estate.

Not only did they change their business model to be a very specific small business lender, they actually proclaim that they are the "Greatest Small Business Lender."

They adopted the strategy with a passion. If a branch didn't have a minimum of 500 small businesses in a three-mile radius, it was closed.

Teller cages were ripped out and replaced with sofas in a family-room-style setting. Customers are greeted with the sensory overload of freshly baked chocolate chip cookies as they enter the branch.

The bank only carries small business inventory, eliminating all consumer-related products: credit cards, overdrafts, real estate mortgages, and car loans.

They cater exclusively to the small business community and have created a knowledge base and culture to win this market niche. When Reines took charge, she knew change was a necessity to ensure the bank's survival.

"We were in a lot of markets that didn't make sense," she says. "We were issuing credit cards and competing with the giants without giving any cash back incentives to our customers. We knew we had to change how we did business.

"It's not the strongest of the species that survives, or the most intelligent, but the one most responsive to change."

She started with a new mission statement: "As the greatest small business bank, First Heritage is passionate about providing financial solutions that enhance value for our customers, shareholders, and community."

Small business lending was the focus for the bank's income stream to be sustainable and critical to building the balance sheet. Retail stores, developers, plant nurseries and restaurants are only a few of the many small businesses that form the heart of First Heritage Bank's customer base.

Larger banks may avoid business loans of less than $250,000, but that's where First Heritage excels, Reines says.

"We've established our niche through years of meeting our small business customers' needs. Whether it means a $15,000 revolving line of credit or a $2 million business opportunity loan, a tradition of resourcefulness and integrity has developed."

Once the bank made the commitment to become the best small business lender they could, she divested the bank of all products that didn't fall under the small business category.

The bank also put an effort into hiring staff who were passionate about small business lending.

"We wanted lenders who could help small businesses be successful. We look for lenders who wake up each morning excited to go to work. We converted our lenders from collateral lenders to cash flow lenders," Reines said.

Cathy will tell you that the employees they attract have a passion for small business lending; when is the last time you heard a banker talk like that?

"We had to shift our mindset that real estate, or collateral, doesn't pay back the loan. It's cash flow."

As a result of Reines' changes, First Heritage increased its SBA lending 100% in 2010, approving $15 million of SBA 7(a) loans. The bank is on pace to become a top 100 SBA 7(a) lender by next year.

Specialty Lenders

Another exciting model is a bank out of Fayetteville, NC—Live Oak Bank. When you meet Annemarie Murphy, the first thing you realize is that she works out of Denver, CO. Technology erases boundries.

When she gives you her card, it will say "Senior Member and Owner." All of the employees at Live Oak own a portion of the bank. The bank has a very narrow small business niche. They only loan to veterinarians and dentists.

They have become experts in this niche, just as that Main Street lender in a farming community in Hills, Iowa was in the 1950s. That bank president knew which farmer worked harder, which farmer yielded the best crops, and which farmer was fiscally conservative.

The banker knew his community, he knew his farmers, and he knew who was the above-average performer whom he could trust.

The same goes for Murphy; since she only deals in two industries, she can quickly size up who is an above-average performer in her industry and who is someone she should shy away from.

One of the themes of this book is that Character is the first C of Credit, and immensely critical. Murphy was one of the first small business lenders who lived and breathed this concept.

Then you have Excel National Bank out of Beverly Hills. Their niche? They will only make loans with a government guaranty, whether it is SBA or a business loan in rural America.

High unemployment figures are a bipartisan concern. Regardless of which side of the aisle you identify with, everyone is in agreement that unemployment figures are too high and the key to economic growth is the creation of jobs.

In rural America, this schism is even bigger.

There are simply too few jobs for youth entering the market, and you continue to see an exodus of rural youth to urban cities. So the USDA developed a program to help mitigate the risk of lending to rural businesses in the form of another government guaranty.

Under president Brian Carlson, Excel National Bank was one of the largest rural lenders of this type in 2010, and they were the fifth-rated lender.

The model of the bank is one of a number of growing banks: use incentives from the federal government in the form of a loan guarantee to mitigate their risk and to get capital to Main Street.

Bill Ruhlman's Borrego Springs Bank is another specialty lender with a slightly different twist in that they exclusively make loans under the SBA Express program.

Now this is a true government partnership, in that the risk is split 50/50 between the taxpayer and the bank.

There is less stress due to regulations and oversight, with the assumption being that if the lender has that much of an exposure, the odds are they will work diligently to protect that exposure as much as the government would.

As an aside, I vehemently reject the idea that the lender will act differently if they have a 90% guaranty versus a 50% guaranty. But unfortunately, that is a common theme by certain politicians and some SBA officials.

In the rare cases of lender fraud, they had nothing to do with the percentage of the guaranty the bank received from the government, but the failure of that bank to catch a rogue employee ripping off the bank.

That rogue employee would have conducted the crime regardless of the guaranty percentage.

Part II: How Banks View You Today

Chapter 6: Character Is the First "C"

Whether you are a banker or a borrower, if you only remember one thing from this book it's that character is the first "C" for the banker.

I'm going to try to define it for you, but you'll quickly find a good definition is elusive. Bankers gave me a lot of different answers, but the one common theme is they know it when they see it.

You can imagine how difficult it is for a lender to judge your character when they first eyeball you from across the desk.

The landscape is littered with businesses, Fortune 500 companies, corner coffee shops, and lenders that have gone bankrupt. You have to convince them that you are smarter than companies like General Motors, CIT, Lehman Brothers, and Joe's Coffee Shop.

Here's one observation about character. It is illegal for banks to consider race in evaluating a loan application. In today's world, there are only idiots who would argue against this premise.

But how do you reconcile the fact that there are a large number of lenders willing to lend a disproportionate share of their hotel loans to the Asian-American community?

I asked around to my lending friends. The explanation?

First, everyone loves the numbers. Loans to the Asian-American community for motels have a very, very low loss rate. It's infinitesimal.

Bankers know these loans get repaid. If there is a problem, the community will step in and work it out.

But isn't this a racial bias, I asked?

No, was the universal response. It's a cultural trait, not a racial trait.

Perhaps they are tap dancing, but here are the facts.

Immigrants from India have found that saving their money and moving to the United States to own and operate a motel is their key to a new life.

And American bankers are willing to help them.

From years of experience bankers have learned that members of this community will work horrendous hours to make the motel successful. And it's a family affair: dad, mom, the kids, uncles, and grandparents all chip in.

If there is a problem they dig deeper in terms of time and commitment. A strong extended family is around to help. The number one character test bankers want to know is that you won't give up.

Character. It's a crucial step in the loan application process. You must convince your banker you have what it takes to succeed.

Coleman Publishing holds an annual conference at Disneyworld every year for small business bankers. I know it's tough duty, but somebody has to do it. We bring in a few hundred lenders and we talk about the industry and the changes within it.

One of my first customers when I began to write the *Coleman Report* in 1993 was Vicki Beaudry of First Coast Community Bank in Jacksonville. Vicki has worked her way up the ranks to where currently she is the executive vice president in charge of small-business lending for the parent company, Synovous Bank.

Speaking at last year's conference, Beaudry made it clear what the "new normal" for lending was: Character comes first. And bluntly, lenders have gotten away from this all-important tenet by focusing exclusively on collateral.

Small business lending didn't quite get itself in the mess that the home lending industry did with liar loans, but as long as you made your benchmarks you could get approved.

Some problems on the credit report? No problem. Waived with an explanation.

If the minimum requirement for a start-up was twenty percent down, bankers wouldn't ask for thirty percent.

Ten percent down to purchase the building on Main Street? Just another check off the checklist and you got your loan.

Character was down at the bottom of the analysis. It was the fifth C.

That's changed.

In her speech, Beaudry referenced an exchange she had recently had with a borrower who had tried to repay his bank loan by turning the property over to the bank.

"Jingle mail" is the term bankers use for these situations.

Jingle mail is more commonly used in reference to residential real estate loans, where the owners simply put the keys into an envelope and send it to the bank, whereupon the keys jingle when the banker opens it up.

But now, small business owners are starting to do the same thing, and the scary part for the lender is the loan might still be current when the business jingle mail comes.

"You know what my response was to that offer?" Beaudry asked the crowd. "That property was never mine to begin with! I gave you money. I want my money back. You can't give me something that I didn't have to begin with."

Vicki clearly understands the new bank model: character is the first C.

"Make sure you know your customer. Don't look at this as a transaction. We are relationship bankers," Beaudry said.

"If I could strike one word from my lender's vocabulary it would be the word 'deal.' There are no deals; there are relationships that we want to build and establish, and these are folks that you will bank with long-term.

"It's a change in your mindset; you're going to make these loans, but you need to know what's in them and if it's something that you are willing to commit to on a long-term basis. Understand your customer's needs in the short-term, with the financing that's going to get them there today, but really get to know them long-term."

The particulars of a potential borrower can change case-by-case, and Beaudry realizes that her community bank philosophies may not apply to all lenders. But the bottom line remains the same.

"I understand that every loan can be structured differently and I'm giving you the perspective of a community bank where we're looking for the deposit relationships, merchant services, and the personal banking needs," Beaudry concluded.

"We're trying to know that customer, know their credit, and finally their collateral. But make sure you get character, then collateral."

Back to the conference room and our new banker watching the Pawn Stars on DVD.

For them, for bankers today, determining character is the most important task. If they purchase an item, or take one in on loan or pawn, and that item is stolen or fake, they lose their entire investment.

This is no different than any other borrower from the bank. If the intention of the borrower is not to pay back the loan, in actuality there is little the bank can do about it.

The Pawn Stars evaluation of character begins as soon as their customer walks through the door. In their business, the Pawn Stars have learned to reserve judgment from visual impressions, preferring to ask the customer a series of questions.

The first question they always ask is a friendly, "Where did you get this?"

The people the Pawn Stars deal with aren't always the most stand-up citizens. The property customers bring in may be stolen or fake. The question of how it came into the customer's possession may seem to be harmless, but the customer's response is critical as to whether negotiations continue.

This is no different than when a banker interviews a borrower. Your conversation starts with an open-ended question, "Tell me what you do and tell me about your business."

The bankers want to know more than about the widgets you sell. They want to get to know you and how you run your business and your life.

Our Pawn Stars do the same analysis. They want to understand if the ownership of the property is valid. Some items are difficult to verify.

Simply based on the emotional attachment that the Pawn Stars can easily read from the holder of the object, family heirlooms passed from mother to daughter are fairly easy to determine if they are owned.

The same is true with the small business banker. Bankers love minutia. The more numbers, facts, and details the borrower has at their fingertips, the more positive signs the banker has that the borrower knows their business.

The Pawn Stars are looking for a story from the customer that makes them believe the customer has legal possession of the item and has knowledge of what it is and its value.

Customers who are terse with their explanations, or tell long, rambling, incoherent stories, or for some reason are puffing themselves up greater than they should, raise an immediate red flag.

Like the Pawn Stars, bankers don't want to be burned. Their bottom line is based on putting cash out and getting it back with minimal hassle.

Essentially, the whole process before the negotiations is the Pawn Stars' way of a background check. They can only go on what they are able to elicit from the customers. A bank will give you a more thorough background check before they approve your loan, but the concept is the same.

In today's economy, bankers are rarely interested in going outside of their footprint—the geographic area where they do their business. Risky deals and gut decisions have now been replaced with accurate projections, double-checked underwriting, and an air of healthy skepticism before approving loans.

A bank has to make loans, but now, more than ever, they won't give them away.

You must do your research and prepare for everything the banker is going to ask for and about. Don't go into the bank without knowing your last month's sales to the dollar. Don't walk in with year-old financial statements.

Don't say, "My CPA has my taxes on extension."

The Five Off-Balance-Sheet Matrices

Small business bankers know that every industry, and every company, has five off-balance-sheet matrices that the entrepreneur knows—should know—cold.

An off-balance-sheet matrix is a key financial number, or fact, that relates directly to the financial health of the company, and they don't show up on your balance sheet or profit and loss statement.

For a restaurant, one matrix could be the average size of the check for the lunch crowd, and is it growing or shrinking? For dinner, is your customer's alcohol consumption up, or down? How many special events do you have planned for next month? What percentage of your sales comes from catering? What are your gross margins on the new buffet you introduced?

For the florist it could be whether Valentine's Day falls on a Sunday (very bad) or a Thursday (very good). What percent of your floral purchases end up in the trash?

Is Home Depot building a new warehouse store three miles away from the mom-and-pop Ace Hardware franchise? Has a major vendor changed their terms from net 30 to COD? What are your sales and profit margins from the Memorial Day sale?

For the doctor, what percentage of her revenues is paid by the patient in cash? How much does it cost in staff time to process a Medicare claim? What is the percentage of insurance company claim rejections, and how long does it take to get your money from the largest provider?

The banker wants to know if you know these numbers and facts, and what you do with them to run your business.

Here are my five numbers that do not show up anywhere on my financial statements, but are a much greater predictor of my future performance than last year's tax return.

1) How many people subscribe to our Coleman Publishing daily emails?

This number fluctuates with people who want to subscribe subtracted by people who want to unsubscribe. The number should always be increasing each day.

Why? Simple marketing. The more emails we send out, the more revenue we receive.

There is a large difference in performance if we send ten thousand emails a day or fifty thousand emails a day. It's one of the first numbers I check each day.

2) While it's important to build an email list, it's more important to write content that motivates my bankers to open up the email. This is the "email open rate." If rates are going down, that means I will have a problem with sales in the following month.

3) The third key matrix for me is the number of visitors that come to our website every day. Again, the more people who come to our website, the more stuff we sell. It's a direct correlation of the numbers.

4) The banker can look at what I sold last year in website advertising from the line item on my profit and loss statement, but that doesn't correlate to what I'll do next month. My scheduled monthly advertising income figure for the following month does. Advertisers come and go, and I need to understand if I'm ahead of last year or behind the curve.

5) My fifth (oh, I have more, but these are my top five) is non-financial. It is the depth of out-product pipeline.

While we have recurring sales from our advertising, renewals of the SBA industry analysis *Coleman Report*, and bankers who attend our conferences each year, our sales growth comes from the introduction of new products—primarily webinars and our small business banker resource publications.

For the webinars we will nab a couple of industry experts and schedule two or three a month on an industry hot topic.

We can estimate the gross revenues from a webinar six weeks out based on the amount of sales we get from our initial marketing campaign.

The same holds true with the sale of our industry data reports and our small business loan underwriting guides.

That helps us to fairly accurately predict our upcoming monthly revenues.

The banker won't know your matrices, but they want to make sure you do. And they want to get a better understanding of your business.

What Other Methods Do Small Business Bankers Use to Evaluate Character?

An understanding of the minutia and an understanding of the off-balance-sheet value of the items is important.

Did you do your assigned homework and Google your name?

Bankers now understand more than ever that Google helps define your character.

When the banker types in your name and an unflattering article pops up, that will be extremely negative to your case.

Understand what is in the cloud out there that describes you!

Those spring break pictures of you in Cancun from college may evoke nice memories, but hardly reinforce your position as a borrower who wants access to someone else's money.

We all understand the concept of anyone can say anything on the web; however, whether it is right or wrong, it is up to you and you have the burden to prove whether it was right or wrong.

Other character tests are old school. In the past, it was important what organizations you belonged to, what country club you belonged to, and the lineage of your mother and father.

Google has replaced that caste system.

Rightly or wrongly, other people will be placing value judgments by the company you keep. And it's all on the web now.

Chamber of commerce mixer picture with that glass of wine in your hand? Fine. PTA? Boy Scouts? Little League? Great. Bankers want you involved in the community.

Church groups? Always helps.

Member of the "Aliens Control the White House" group? Uh oh.

Ask Christine O'Donnell how the character debate worked in her Delaware Senate race when she revealed her "experimentation" with witchcraft.

Character counts. Character is important.

Character Documents

A standard measurement of a person's character used to be their FICO credit score.

That has changed in today's lending environment as well. Notice that the Pawn Stars aren't concerned with a potential customer's credit score; they are only concerned with whether the product was obtained legally and does the person in front of them have the legal ability to offer the item for sale.

But even this basic test was lost. Look at what got us into the subprime mortgage crisis.

Bankers lent money to people who may have had the legal ability to offer their home as collateral but certainly did not have the financial ability, the character, or the willingness to pay back that debt.

Having a partner or a spouse is problematic. Not only must you convince the lender of your sterling character, you will also be aligned with the character and the credit score of your partner or spouse.

In the SBA loan application (Form 912), there has always been a three-question personal history test:

1. Are you presently under indictment, on parole or probation?

2. Have you ever been charged with and or arrested for any criminal offense other than a minor motor vehicle violation? Include offenses which have been dismissed, discharged, or not prosecuted.

3. Have you ever been convicted, placed on pretrial diversion, or placed on any form of probation; including adjudication withheld pending probation, for any criminal offense other than a minor vehicle violation?

Of course, from this wording a lot of people are caught in this web. Have you ever been arrested? It's embarrassing when someone has to explain a "youthful transgression."

Many people object to the question, but unfortunately it is one of those "cash is king" rules.

He who has cash is king, and the king makes the rules.

If the borrower is offended by the question, they don't have to answer it and they can withdraw their application. If your spouse or partner has a problem, the best defense is offense.

Full transparency and full documentation. If one partner was arrested for stealing in 1993, you should come prepared with a sheaf of papers stapled, and hand it over saying that this explains that problem and here is the resolution. You will never get into trouble for providing too much information.

Spouses are trickier; some lenders will require the financials and the personal guaranty of the spouse. Have those conversations early with your spouse and make sure they know the full expectations of what that lender needs; you don't want to be negotiating with the lender whether he or she needs to sign line number 37.

This shows tremendous weakness in the application process. You may have convinced the banker of your willingness to ride out any storm, but if you have a spouse or partner who simply refused to put their name on a piece of paper, red flags are going to pop up in the lender's mind.

"What Is Character?"

Preparing for a speech I gave before a group of small business bankers in Maine last year, I again tried to define character.

I went "new" school.

I took out my iPhone and interviewed small business owners and bankers on what their definition of character was.

I got varying answers, but certain themes were clear.

Honesty ranked first. Being honest with both the customer and honest with yourself on what you promise you can back up.

For the banker, the belief that the person has the intentional fortitude to pay the lender back, no matter what obstacles are encountered, is the common theme.

I wanted to learn more.

Back to specialty lender Live Oak Bank—the veterinarian and dentist lender.

The good news in lending to animal doctors and dentists is that these loans are paid back at a higher rate than other small business loans.

The bad news is that a medical license is not an automatic ticket for success.

Some loans go bad, and when they do there is a higher loss percentage because there is not as much collateral as with other loans.

These tend to be "cash flow" loans and are based on the ability of the professional to generate fees to support a practice.

Senior lender Annemarie Murphy went back through her loan portfolio to see if there was a common thread with her problem credits.

She analyzed loans and made a list. She wanted to learn from her bank's past mistakes.

And she got creative.

Playing off of the five Cs, she calls her list the five Ds.

Murphy's five Ds that can end any medical professional practice are: Death, Disability, Drugs, Depression, and Divorce.

Lenders must get an in-depth understanding of their borrowers' professional practices and lifestyles.

For example, in a single-doctor practice, if the physician dies, the entire practice may end.

If the lender believes the death of one person will jeopardize your business, plan on buying insurance to protect them in case you end up on the wrong side of a bus accident.

The second D is the potential disability of the owner.

A dentist may break a wrist or a couple of fingers skiing and lose some mobility or motility. This may require a transition from a clinical practice into a teaching practice, resulting in a 20% to 40% revenue reduction.

With such a steep decline in income, could the dentist still repay the loan?

The stress level for doctors and dentists tends to be very high. Whether from litigation, government reform, or the pressures of running a practice as a business, stress can contribute to depression.

The fact that doctors can write their own prescriptions to ease their depression can, and has, lead to incidents of drug use and abuse. This one is a little tough for lenders to figure out, but Murphy demands her loan officers spend a half day with a borrower onsite to get a better understanding of the person behind the signature.

A cursory tour of the practice and a conversation over a long lunch can provide insight.

Vets and dentists are people like everyone else.

Divorce is a major setback in any medical professional's or small business owner's life. They tend to be bitter, unpleasant, and costly.

Tom Wallace runs a certified development company in Ft. Myers, Florida—ground zero of the financial crisis.

He shrewdly points out that a staff that is extremely attractive increases the risk of divorce exponentially!

Note that plastic surgeons are exempt from this rule since advertising pays—beautiful people draw patients who want to become beautiful!

In preparing your loan application, spend the greatest amount of time of addressing the banker's character concerns.

Fire the consultant you've hired to prepare your business plan. Instead, prepare an outline of talking points to convince your banker why you are in the top ten percent of those who have walked through their door today.

What is character?

You know it when you see it.

Chapter 7: How Exactly Does Cash Flow Repay Loans?

In lending, the first C is character. The second is cash flow.

Let me give you the math on how a banker looks at your business from a cash flow standpoint.

If you have a business, pull out last year's tax return.

If you're planning one, take out your projections.

Start with the bottom line—your profit before tax.

The acronym is EBITD (Earnings Before Interest Taxes & Depreciation). It's a serious number. Don't even go down the road with the banker that the figure on your tax return is different from reality.

Bankers and their regulators pay their taxes and they think you should also.

When you imply that you make more profit than is shown on your tax return it will get you the same response Harrison Ford's character got when he claimed innocence to Tommy Lee Jones's U.S. marshal character in *The Fugitive*.

Remember the scene? Jones says in a very slow, low, staccato voice, "I….. don't….. care."

For bankers and regulators there are only two reasons you don't pay taxes, and both are bad.

Either you haven't made any money, or you are a crook.

If you want a ticket to the dance, you have to pay the price. More on this later.

Now, take your profit before tax and add to that number what you paid on interest and for income taxes.

Then add that line called depreciation.

That is how bankers define the cash you brought in last year.

Now start subtracting.

Deduct all your loan payments—principal and interest.

Deduct what the new loan payment will cost you.

If you have more cash than deductions, the bank deems you have positive cash flow.

And they want a coverage ratio. The higher the better. In today's lending environment you need to be at a minimum 125% coverage on average for the past three years.

Now, there are a variety of iterations of this calculation, and the good news is I'm not going to expound on them. Let the purists do that.

I just want you to have a general theory on what the bank is looking for and hopefully put you in the ballpark.

Just as everyone agrees the global climate is changing, there are fierce debates on the cause and action for solutions. The same hold true with the bankers' concept of cash flow.

I am an off-road Jeep enthusiast and have spent many weekends driving through Death Valley and the deserts of the Southwest.

I've come across dinosaur tracks left in what were lush swampy jungles that are now fossilized on high desert buttes. I've driven in expansive breathtaking remote valleys that were once submerged under thousands of feet of ocean water.

The evidence clearly proves the earth's climate has changed. I'm just confused about whether our caveman ancestors' cooking fires had anything to do with it.

Bankers have a similar problem when it comes to figuring out if an entrepreneur will repay his or her small business loan.

They obviously need a better model than they've used in the past.

You're beginning to see the evolution of a new model beginning with the emphasis on character.

But, back to cash flow.

I asked a banking friend about cash flow and how a banker determines if the borrower has enough cash to repay the loan. I was given the formula.

I interrupted him, "But how about the cash reserves on the financial statement? Isn't that part of a company's cash flow?"

That stumped him and he said, "Well, I suppose the $50 million Microsoft has in reserves helps."

He was wrong. Not about cash on hand boosting the cash flow numbers, but how much Microsoft had in the bank.

Microsoft's cash reserves are $50 billion with a "b."

Ok, ok, you caught me, they're really at $40 billion, but I'm being like my mom, not letting facts get in the way of a good story.

That puts them fourth on the top-twenty list of corporations with the largest cash reserves.

The top spot belongs to Warren Buffet's Berkshire-Hathaway, whose cash holdings in his subsidiaries are estimated to be around $150 billion. General Electric is second at over $100 billion. Ford Motor Company, which pays taxes, rounds out the top at about $50 billion.

Now, some suggest the way out of the recession is simply to have corporations spend the money they are hoarding.

The argument is government stimulus functions differently than corporate stimulus. And that if the greedy and unpatriotic corporations would just get off the dime and loosen up the coin purse we'll be back on the right track in no time.

The flaw in this misguided argument, of course, is that governments can print money.

Corporations can't.

How are large corporations managing their survival through the recession? The answer is simple. The answer is cash.

But spending money simply for the sake of spending money hasn't necessarily worked out for the government. The only downside to this course of action is we will have exponentially higher debt, and we will have to handle the higher interest with that debt.

A private company that spends money for the sake of spending money will be bankrupt. Banks that loan money for the sake of loaning money will be bankrupt.

Hoarding cash is not anti-Obama, or even anti-American. It is simply a managerial decision that if a company has cash in the bank, they are guaranteed to survive.

Similarly, it is irresponsible to attack banks for hoarding cash, because they have the same mentality. Cash is penance and absolves a number of sins.

Hmmm, I seem to have digressed.

The reason why a bank does its cash flow analysis on the borrower is they want the answer to the question, "Will you be able to pay back the loan?"

Why Does a Small Business Fail?

I've said the reason why small businesses fail is the owner finally gives up.

Obviously, not having cash in the bank helps that decision.

To succeed, the entrepreneur must understand their small business's cash flow to the penny. More importantly, the entrepreneur must understand what increases and decreases that cash flow, and be able to convey that to the lender.

The first part of understanding cash flow is to understand where cash comes from.

Now I know you are rolling your eyes and thinking I'm talking down to you, but consider this: If I walked into your office and you had ten thousand dollars in cash sitting on your desk, I can assure you that your number one priority at that time would be to take the necessary precautions to protect the cash and lock it up in a safe place.

But do you treat your sources of cash the same?

You must.

You need to treat your accounts receivable with that same attitude. If people owe you money, you need to manage that process daily. You need to clearly understand when you will be receiving that cash.

If someone agrees to pay you in thirty days, and you agree to the terms, state up front you are not in the business of chasing dollars and you expect payment on time.

If you don't have the payment on the thirtieth day, you must make the call. I know it's unpleasant.

If you don't want to do it, then have someone do it for you. You can hire a freelancer or a virtual assistant to do this one function if you are too small to afford a full-time bookkeeper.

If you have inventory, do everything you can do keep the amount at a minimum without sacrificing the soul of your business.

Coleman Publishing sells books, but you won't see any in our office. We use a print-on-demand service that can drop ship our books anywhere in the world. Not having any inventory frees up a lot of cash for us.

Don't be afraid to ask for deposits and favorable terms upfront. Don't minimize the fact that you have sold your customer on your product. And they want to do business with you.

If you sell on account, alter your terms. Demand credit card numbers up front, and for the file. We've had success using PayPal.

Bankers are skittish at handing out their credit card information. We'll send them an email as an invoice. They input their credit card information and we never see it, which is fine by me.

The bonus is that we get the money in our account immediately. Unlike banks who won't give you credit for checks for one day, or merchant credit card deposits for two or three days.

Be aggressive on getting upfront deposits. Get financing from the people who want your stuff.

That's how I started my business. When I started the *Coleman Report* in 1993 I charged $395 for an annual subscription.

Upfront. I found out the banks would pay and I haven't looked back since.

Consider this: If you are late on your obligations, by one day, say your credit card, the bank will think nothing of charging you a $39 late fee and raising your rate from 7% to 29%.

I know from personal experience.

I have a line of credit with Citi. For some strange reason the bank changed my address and sent my bill to that other address. The next month, I didn't get a bill.

I wasn't paying particularly close attention to my obligation and I never realized I had missed the payment.

Well, I got a call for being late from a really nice lady (an anomaly in the world of bank credit collectors) and she wanted to know why I wasn't paying my little bill to a bank that had been bailed out with $50 billion in TARP money?

OK, she didn't mention TARP (I again embellish), but we squared away the address problem. I made a payment by phone and moved on with everyday life.

So I thought. You know where this is going.

Got my statement the following month with the little notation my interest rate had been raised to 29% because I had missed the payment.

Wow.

A phone call solved the problem, but the moral of the story is that if you are treated this way by your lender, you can probably be a little bit more aggressive with the people who owe you money and still be able to live with yourself.

Don't forget that your customers need you as much as you need them. If you are a good vendor who provides good service, you can afford to stretch the terms of your relationship a little bit.

True, they can go somewhere else, but there is a cost for them to leave you. Just as there is a cost for you to leave your bank.

Again, sorry to be repetitive, but you need to understand every source of cash, not just the people who walk in through the door and plunk it down on the counter.

If you don't believe me, add up all the money that is due you in accounts receivable, from everyone who owes you money.

If that figure were sitting in your bank account, wouldn't you be sleeping better tonight?

Enough of the lecture.

Just convert as much of your accounts receivable to cash as possible. You didn't get a bail out. Have your customers borrow the money from those that did, and get you paid up front, or at a minimum on time.

This attention to detail on cash inflows is also required for cash outflows—but try to *delay* as long as possible.

Except the IRS. It's always wise to first pay those who carry guns and operate prisons. I'd pay them before your mob loan. The interest is about the same for delinquencies. Both have excellent collection systems.

But if your knees get broken—well, that's why you have health insurance.

Extended delinquency to the IRS will get you an extended vacation. Ask Wesley Snipes, or the poor sap who won the first "Survivor" competition.

In today's climate don't even walk through the door of a bank if you have an unpaid payroll tax problem. You will have no success in explaining an IRS lien in today's climate.

Not gonna fly.

I was asked the other day about burn rates, and whether it is acceptable for a start-up business to spend cash like the government until they break even.

The answer is this: of course, if you like skydiving while trying to put on your parachute!

Some will make it, but the outcome for most is predictable.

A better analogy is setting aside cash for the introduction of new products.

I don't gamble. Not because I have a problem; I just don't like the odds. I'm gambling every week with my business cash flow.

And those odds are much better and the results can be much more satisfying.

For example, in our business we do a number of webinars and conferences. We reach our customers through email promotions and ads on our website.

Those ads are our storefront and our face in the industry. We can only promote one or two items at a time, as there is a cost in generating advertising copy, inviting speakers, and setting up the event.

But the bigger risk is the opportunity cost of choosing the wrong program. If we choose poorly, we not only lose the cost, the burn, of the venture, we also lose what we would have made on a more successful event.

We're a lot smarter than we were several years ago.

As I said, in the first twenty-four hours of announcing an event we can tell how popular or unpopular it will be by the sales generated. Call this benchmark our own exit poll data.

If we don't get sufficient traction, we'll eat our loss and kill the event. Quickly.

We're ruthless on this. We stopped a long time ago trying to fit a square peg into a round hole.

Appropriate Methods of Cash Flow

In your traditional MBA school, you are taught the two things that eat up cash are an increase in inventory and an increase in accounts receivable.

It's the classic reason why a company needs a loan.

There was some talking head on TV during the height of the Great Recession who was pontificating about how Main Street credit wasn't all that important.

"Why does Main Street need credit anyway?" he solemnly intoned. If it's a viable business it won't need to borrow money!

I'm surprised how much I am able to restrain myself from hurling stuff at my TV.

Of course it's fine for Fortune 500 companies to have debt to build stuff, for the US government to have debt, for Wall Street to have debt to continue to operate, and for the American consumer to have debt to buy a house or a car, but if a small business has debt, it's a sign of irresponsibility.

Let's go through it a step at a time as to why a small business on Main Street needs capital.

Inventory.

Their inventory, whatever it is, must be created.

If you are a manufacturer, your inventory is produced by a combination of labor, raw materials, and the overhead that turns on the lights and provides water to the restrooms for your employees.

All that costs money.

The florist buys her flowers from a wholesaler. But she must have someone put them in a vase, buy the vase and ribbon, and pay for electricity to run the refrigerator. The flower arrangement is inventory until it can be sold. If it doesn't sell immediately, it's all a loss and it's thrown into the trash, the fee for which must be paid on time every month to get picked up.

Service companies have inventory also.

An attorney talks to a client—that's his time. He then instructs an assistant to prepare a piece of paper. That paper is picked up by a courier and filed at the court. That process is inventory.

Everyone who touches that process wants to be paid. Labor is paid weekly. The electric and water companies want their money monthly.

Staples wants money upfront before they will ship you paper. Your QuickBooks accounting system on the cloud needs its $24.95 each month up front. Airlines like getting their money *months* before you fly.

Oh, and all the various government agencies who are taxing you want their money, on time, no delay, no questions asked.

On the other side of the coin is the cash you bring in. It's variable. Hopefully your customers pay in thirty days. For others, as in the example of the attorney, it could be months. Wal-Mart, I'll get to them later, pays you 120 days.

Remember the days when American Express wouldn't pay its merchants for thirty days after you submitted them your customer's charge slip?

Small business owners aren't consumers with a weekly paycheck. Their cash outflows don't always sync nicely with their cash inflows.

That's why Main Street needs credit.

Let's look at the numbers in this example.

Say you are a manufacturer producing widgets, and you purchase $50,000 of material and contract $50,000 for labor. Your cost is $100,000. (Of course accountants want an overhead calculation, but let's not confuse ourselves.)

Your employees want to be paid right away so you're immediately out $50,000 for the month.

But you negotiate terms with your supplier, and since your supplier has read this book they adhere to a daily management of cash flow. They've made it clear they don't chase dollars and they expect—demand!—payment in thirty days.

Fortunately you are shrewd and you've sold your widgets for $125,000.

However, since your buyer says he won't get *his* money for thirty days, he can't pay you until forty-five days. And it takes a week to ship your stuff.

And a week to get the check.

You're out $100,000 in thirty days. And you get $125,000—the money you have generated from your $100,000 investment—in sixty days.

So this is why Main Street needs credit. Without $100,000 in credit, there is no order, no profit, and no employees.

Bankers want to know this cycle. They'll want to know if you are taking that money for other purposes.

While the phrase "working capital" is easy to understand as a catch-all term, the banker wants to know the money is not going into a black hole and making up for past failures.

Every small business has skeletons in the closet when it comes to debt. You can quickly add up the day's financial drain on the company and see that our company is no exception.

We have an old vendor account on which we owe $1,000. We haven't paid it off. Why? We're like Warren Buffet. We're conserving cash. And the vendor hasn't read this book. I haven't received one call.

At some point in time we'll make an accommodation with the vendor and pay it off—perhaps at a discount.

The banker doesn't want to hear this. They want to make sure their money, their inventory, isn't being used to pay off past sins.

If you walk into your community bank and say you want $250,000 to pay off your Bank of America credit line, you better have a better reason for doing so than you simply want to change banks. In today's environment they know you are being asked to leave.

Here's the important takeaway: don't pay retail! If the banker perceives that you don't understand the value of cash (and remember cash is king), you must convince them you do and that you know cash leads any transaction.

In the previous case (a business trying to get a $250,000 loan from the bank), you will be much more successful by having the previous bank term that debt for a period of five to seven years.

Getting a bank to write you a check for $250,000 is very difficult; you're better off conserving that cash for future business opportunities that you can purchase at a discount, rather than simply refinancing existing debt.

Remember, I also said that any increase in assets eats up cash. Conversely, any increase in liability is also a source of cash.

There are a number of reasons why I hate Wal-Mart and this is one. Those small businesses who are unfortunate enough to land a contract with Wal-Mart risk selling their souls like Joe Hardy in the old classic *Damn Yankees*.

Wal-Mart's average accounts payable turn is well over ninety days from the invoice date.

This means Wal-Mart is borrowing from its vendors.

You don't like the terms, fine, Wal-Mart will go somewhere else.

Any business that allows for Wal-Mart to be a major source of their revenue—say anything over ten percent—has found only fool's gold.

They simply become employees (although sometimes very well-paid employees but still, employees) of Wal-Mart and their business is fully controlled by Wal-Mart. Wal-Mart is their Old Man.

When Wal-Mart comes in for their annual review and squeezes your small business's profits, you have to understand the devil you are married to. Wal-Mart sales are over a billion dollars *per day* (yes, billion with a "b"), but even they clearly understand the need for cash reserves.

If these entities are sitting on cash, it would behoove the small business entrepreneur to follow their lead. This also breeds confidence with the banker. If you walk into the bank with $100,000 cash to open an account and then you ask for a $20,000 credit line, I can assure you the banker will feel all warm and fuzzy about your venture.

Bankers do not like high-maintenance customers. If you are calling the bank every day to see which checks have cleared, then rushing in to cover those checks with 3:00 pm deposit, you are not going to build a lasting foundation for success.

Now, I'm not talking about the occasional indiscretion; there will always be glitches, and only small business entrepreneurs know the terror of trying to meet Friday's payroll when they are looking at a significant five-figure deficit Thursday evening.

It is in those "what should be" rare instances, where a good banking relationship can literally save your company.

A friend of mine named Richard Oshoff runs a similar publication to mine for the legal sector, Stratford Publications out of Atlanta. Several years ago we were at an executive retreat for newsletter publishers in Chicago.

Someone was droning on about the importance of market testing and how by tweaking the structure of this email or that direct mail, by moving a line here, or putting a little picture there, you can add an additional return.

And while this was all interesting, it was extremely theoretical for smaller publishers such as us.

The presentation continued and the presenter droned on, "Now this is really important stuff because it can get you an extra two tenths of one percent return."

Finally Richard had enough of the how many angels can dance on the head of a test marketing email piece discussion. "Look, I don't think that long-term. All I know is that I go into the office in the morning and the first thing I do is to check the bank account. If we have money we're good to work that day."

Richard understands cash is king. And while all of these others issues are important, at the end of the day it's the companies with cash in the bank that operate.

How Do Bankers Calculate Cash Flow?

As I've mentioned, I gave a keynote speech to a variety of east coast lenders in Portland, Maine last year. The title of the speech was "Character is the First C." And I challenged the lenders with this question:

"Where did we buy into the theory that past historical performance will make future loan payments?"

I told the lenders of my unusual undergraduate degree in Medieval History, and that it taught me the foundations for my banking career. That usually draws a laugh, but in reality what that degree taught me was how to read and write. It also taught me how to think critically.

Here's the example I offered why the banking industry needs to change its reliance on historical cash flow.

The evaluation of a venture based on the assumption everything will perform as it did in the past has proven to be fatally flawed. Again, small business failure rates are exhibit A.

History also teaches us why unexpected outcomes are more common than we might think.

The performance of the American ice hockey team over the Soviets at the 1980 Lake Placid Olympics is one classic example.

But my favorite example of how you can't use past performance to predict future performance is when 30,000 French defeated an Islamic army of 80,000 and stopped the 200-year Islamic expansion from the Middle East.

In 732 AD the French king Charles Martel assembled a rag-tag band of Frankish farmers on top of a hill in north central France to confront Abdul Rahman Al Ghafiqi and his Islamic army, which had left what is now modern Spain and was driving through Europe.

Up until this point in European history the Islamic religion had steadily conquered and converted populations throughout the Middle East, North Africa, and southern Spain.

Al Ghafiqi had won many skirmishes and battles, and was seeking to convert the rest of Europe to Islam. His army, the Umayyad Caliphate, hadn't lost a battle in two hundred years, and was composed of 80,000 experienced and highly trained soldiers.

Based on past historical performance of 200 years on winning battles by the Islamic army, and the fact Martel was outnumbered almost three to one, and had never commanded an army into battle, no one would have given him a chance to succeed.

Frankly—yep, pun intended—if Charles Martel had not shockingly defeated Al Ghafiqi, the debate by some of whether Europe or the United States should incorporate Sharia law would have been settled fourteen centuries ago.

Many historians agree this one battle was the most significant historical event of the past 2,000 years.

Here's what happened:

Al Ghafiqi and his army marched into a field in northern France and stumbled upon Martel and his troops. Martel had the higher ground, but at the time only about 15,000 soldiers.

If Al Ghafiqi had decided to attack that day, he would have won the battle, but not knowing exactly how many men where in the Frankish army he decided to set up camp and wait.

After a couple of days, Al Ghafiqi had a problem. He had 80,000 soldiers, thousands of horses, wagons full of loot acquired in victories from his march from Spain, and the usual camp "followers" that swelled his numbers.

But there was no food.

In order to travel light, Al Ghafiqi and his army lived off of the land. After seven days of camping and figuring out what Martel was up to, well, let's just say it wasn't a good time to be a deer in France.

Also, it was getting cold. Winter was coming and his army didn't have winter clothes.

After a week, these factors began to force Al Ghafiqi's hand towards the decision to attack.

Meanwhile, Martel had sent word—more like screamed for help—and had gotten tens of thousands of farmers, peasants and serfs to run to his aid.

Now, let me clarify.

Martel had foreseen and prepared for this battle for twenty years. He'd built and maintained the small army of 15,000 fighting men. He paid to have them outfitted with the best swords and armor of the day.

But the French army hadn't exactly put together a track record that would give Al Ghafiqi pause.

All Martel had was 15,000 fighting men, the 15,000 farmers, and the high ground.

When Al Ghafiqi finally decided to attack, he correctly assumed he outnumbered the French and thought he could intimidate them. He was correct about the size of his opponent's army, but he sorely misjudged his ability to intimidate Martel and his troops.

Al Ghafiqi began by having his cavalry attack the center of Martel's line, the intent being to overwhelm them with force until it broke.

But, Martel was entrenched with the proper pole defenses—we're talking twenty-foot spikes that could kill a horse and man and not be touched. The cavalry's first charge failed.

Al Ghafiqi wasn't deterred. Knowing that he had the upper hand in terms of numbers, he sent his entire army to the center of Martel's line. No reserves.

Like Pickett at Gettysburg a millennium later, everybody advanced.

It was a bloody massacre. Both sides were taking heavy losses in the hand-to-hand fighting. Martel's center of the line was holding, but it would only be a matter of time before the overwhelming numbers of Islamic forces prevailed.

Except the unexpected happened.

Martel, with no military training and little military experience, performed the maneuver that changed the course of world history.

While he held the line against Al Ghafiqi's murderous attack, he sent a small contingent of raiders to the back of the Islamic lines, which had been left unguarded.

The raiders helped themselves to the loot, slaves, and women.

Then all hell broke loose.

The word quickly spread to Al Ghafiqi's troops that the loot they'd fought so hard for was being stolen.

They broke off the attack and headed back to camp.

Martel's cavalry weren't fools. They grabbed the loot and some women and hightailed it out of there before Al Ghafiqi's army caught them.

The breakdown of Al Ghafiqi's lines spread his troops out over the battlefield.

Martel attacked what was now the rear of Al Ghafiqi's army and mowed them down. In the scrum, trying to rally his army, Al Ghafiqi was killed.

That was it. With their leader dead, the battle was over. The Islamic army retreated, packed up what was left of their belongings and headed back to Spain.

This would become the high-water mark of Islam's reach into Europe. Charles Martel earned the nickname "Charles the Hammer," and sired another lasting legacy on Western Europe.

This one you may know: his grandson was Charlemagne, who became the founder of the Holy Roman Empire.

If you had based your expectations on the outcome of the Battle of Tours based on previous experience, no one would have given the French (yes, the French!) a fighting chance.

This is the challenge I gave to the bankers.

Historical cash flow numbers don't pay back loans. Past performance is not necessarily a predictor of future performance.

It's the willingness and ability of the small business owner to write that check to the bank each month that pays back loans.

Cash Is King

Cash is king. As with everything, what I learned during my studies at USC was vastly different than what I learned on the street. I learned that it isn't branding or market share or price/earning multiples; it is simply if there is enough cash in the bank to keep the lights on.

Excellent business authors have tried to explain what makes a business successful. Tom Peters is the first to come to mind.

One definition of character is the ability to manage a small business, or any business, at an excellent operating level.

When I attempted to find a definition of character, I went to Main Street to talk to small business owners who had not only survived the Great Recession, but were optimistic about the future.

In 1978, when I was a newly minted junior commercial lending officer, one of the loan applications that crossed my desk was for a new flower shop in the burgeoning Simi Valley, a growing suburb in Los Angeles.

Frank and Katie Mutal ran a flower shop in Northridge, California, and had wanted to construct a building for their son to open his own floristry. The business, Michael's Flowers, has now been in the community for over thirty years.

But, business success is not a Woody Allen line of "opening the doors 90% of the time."

It takes a little bit more than that.

When asked about how he defines character, the first response from Michael Mutal was honesty.

Michael acknowledges to his customers that he and his employees aren't perfect, and that mistakes will be made. But, he assures them that they will be corrected and prevented in the future.

Another family-owned business is a Firestone franchise operation in La Cañada. Dave Bobzin is your stereotypical barrel-chested, good-ole-boy auto mechanic. He and his father have operated the franchise also for thirty years.

When asked for his definition of character, he sheds his auto-mechanic persona, and clearly enunciates what a big business would call a mission statement, or in the jargon of the day, his elevator pitch.

"We are here to build everything for repeat business. You can't build everything for today's business or today's sales. We focus on being honest and treating people well, and if you do that, they'll come back in the bad times."

Small business ownership is difficult. There are reasons why there is a very high failure rate. The small business owner must be a Renaissance man or woman.

They must become experts in branding, marketing, accounting, production, human resources, sales, advertising, and economics.

The failure to understand and perform even one of these tasks can lead to the business's demise.

When I started Coleman Publishing in 1993, I had the romantic, idealistic view that I would be sitting in my underwear at the kitchen table writing a trade newsletter.

Obviously, the reality is different from perception. First of all, writing is difficult.

Stephen King, the prolific writer of classics such as *The Shining* and *The Green Mile*, has a great line when people ask him the secret to his proficiency.

He simply stares back and answers, "I just sit down and write."

Easier said than done.

I was also ahead of the curve with a home-based business, but you must be very disciplined and dedicated to deal with the isolation and produce a viable work product.

Another thing no one ever told me was that not only did you have to put in eight, ten, and twelve-hour days, but you had to be smart in your decision making. I found that about once every three months I would be faced with a decision that if I chose poorly would end my venture.

Fortunately today we are in a more stable situation, but those same concepts apply.

Misjudging partnership opportunities, not paying attention to your brand, or failing to deliver products as your customers evolve, can all be deadly sins.

However, big business hasn't done any better than small business in the past.

The incredible decision by Circuit City to fire all of their higher-paid sales personnel is one such example. Call it "death by spreadsheet-itis."

Some idiotic bean counter said that if Circuit City were able to reduce its payroll expenses, the reduction would automatically increase the company's bottom line.

So, Circuit City fired all of their longer tenured employees, and assumed that the customer would buy the same product from a $10/hr worker as they would a $20/hr worker.

Customers fled Circuit City stores in droves because the inexperienced and incompetent sales staff didn't know a cell phone from a TV set.

The Circuit City board of directors surely realized their mistake when they signed the bankruptcy papers.

As Bob Brady, a successful newsletter publisher of BLR Compliance Information, said, "Our information is sold, not bought." He clearly understands the need to articulate the benefits of his products to his customers.

Kevin Finch runs a high-end restaurant in La Cañada, California called Dish.

Ahead of his time, he promotes the concept of buying from local farmers.

No one could spell carbon footprint five years ago. Today it's the rage, so much so that United Airlines lists being green as its first priority, over safety and customer service.

Everyone knows the restaurant business is tough. If there is a shift in your customer base, by the time you figure that out, you're already dead in the water.

But Kevin Finch has his formula down. He is an expert in the local demographics. He understands the difference between his breakfast, lunch, and dinner crowds, and tailors the menus and pricing for all three crowds.

He is no different from the Quiznos franchise owner who understands the value of ten-percent-discount coupons to his bottom line.

He is an expert in using the spreadsheet to forecast predicted outcomes, and he understands the unintended consequences of adjusting one cell on the whole model.

One of the underlying themes in our discussions with Main Street business owners is when we ask them that question they aren't stumped.

They immediately have an answer.

It's like with the aww-shucks-good-ole'-boy mechanic Dave Bobzin—you are flipping a switch and they go into a corporate business mode. But you can tell from the heartfelt responses that these are not canned speeches or rehearsed sound-bites; they are the framework of their ideology.

And they know cash is king.

Chapter 8:
The Rest of the Five "C's"

The importance of the first two C's, Character and Cash Flow, are obvious, but that does not minimize the value of the remaining C's: Capital, Collateral, and Conditions.

Just as a failure to have the appropriate character or cash flow will doom a small business venture, a failure in any of the remaining C's will lead to a similar outcome.

The simple answer to the question of what the lender wants from you in terms of collateral is simply this: everything.

Just as Columbus burned his boats when he reached the New World to encourage his sailors to adapt to the local environment, the lender wants similar assurances that you are appropriately motivated to make your business a success and overcome any known or unforeseen obstacles.

Make no mistake—small business lenders have learned the painful lesson that collateral does not repay loans. But that doesn't mean they won't take it.

Capital

Third on our list of the five C's is capital, which is the amount of cash you accumulate to support your business venture. (It doesn't have to be *your* cash; capital includes the cash that you raise from the three F's: Friends, Family, and Fools. We'll talk about that later.).

Capital includes all potential sources of cash: spousal, or I guess I should say significant other income; liquidation of 401k plans; even potential inheritance and future pension payments.

It's not very scientific, but it helps to paint a picture for the banker to understand the extent of your potential liquidity.

One of the lessons learned by bankers in the past couple of years is the ability (or rather the inability) of their customers to convert their personal assets to cash.

The residential ATM disappeared, 401k values dropped precipitously, and even business valuations dropped tremendously. Of course, the values of their businesses had a corresponding decline in valuation.

Raw experience has forced lenders to critically eye your financial statements at entirely new levels.

If you think your house is worth $400,000 and you owe the bank $200,000, you may believe you have $200,000 in equity.

Not so fast!

Today, the banker will give you little credit for that equity. Oh, they'll take your house as collateral for your business loan—that hasn't changed—it's just that you will not get as much credit as before.

Like the gold miners of the Yukon found, it may be one thing to own a claim full of gold. It's an entirely different matter to extract the gold and convert it to cash.

Here are some impediments that are obvious to your banker. Credit has tightened. In recent years, home equity lenders have canceled hundreds of billions of dollars of home equity lines. And you need a place to live—you simply can't turn your home equity into a liquid asset.

Even if you sell your home for $400,000 and take your equity, you have to move somewhere else. Even if you can decide to downsize, or rent, which will trigger paying capital gains, there is no scenario that will be able for you to convert 100% of your home equity into cash.

There are transaction fees—on a $400,000 home sale, real estate brokerage fees of six percent add up to $24,000. There are loan prepayment fees, and repair and maintenance costs in preparing the property for sale.

Don't forget to add in moving costs.

And we haven't even begun to talk about the costs in acquiring the new property. Even if you choose to rent you're going to be writing a check for a couple of months' worth of rent and a deposit. Plus more deposits to turn on the water and electricity.

What's left of your IRA and 401k may be a nice number, but it isn't cash. There are tax consequences for conversion.

And don't think your pension is safe. Lenders read the papers. If your pension is from the state of California it will be discounted appropriately.

The purity of the Pawn Star transaction is that it reflects a true equity price.

You have the option to consign something to auction or list it on eBay. But if you want cash—to get paid hundred dollar bills *today*—you quickly come to find true value.

The measurement of capital is your real access to cash. If you need it, how much can you truly get?

Which brings us to shiny objects: boats, airplanes, artwork, sports cars, the cabin in the woods.

All of these are symbols of affluence. You may think that your capital worth on your personal financial statement is enhanced with the inclusion of such toys.

Sorry—there is nothing further from the truth.

While your golfing banker buddy may enjoy his membership at the local country club, odds are it is a perk and paid for by the bank.

Your membership will be viewed as a drain on your capital.

We've talked about the hierarchy of the bank, and at the very top are the regulators. Regulators will never meet you. They don't know about your charisma and they don't know of your ability to inspire confidence in all of those around you.

All they know is that the cabin in the woods and the small plane you've bought to ferry you and your family there to do a little hunting and fishing don't show someone of affluence, but rather an individual who has toys and also must obtain financing for his business.

The two are incompatible in the black-and-white worldview of the regulator.

Regulators, and of course their bankers, want you to behave as they do. I've talked to regulators (some of whom are my best friends) and when they buy the RV, they buy it at a 50% discount, with cash, no financing, at a foreclosure auction.

They expect the same of you.

Bankers, as we've said, are in the mode of *accumulating* cash. They are not taking that cash and buying private jets and villas in Italy.

Well, there was that one case in Georgia of a banker using bank funds to buy a private jet and a couple villas in Florida, but that guy is now looking at real estate in the federal penal system.

I'm not saying you can't have your toys. What I'm saying is that you need to understand those aren't positives. They are negatives and you must downplay them as much as possible.

You must disclose it on your personal financial statement, but if you bought a property for $50,000 in 1992, I would certainly not put down the $500,000 valuation that your neighbor's property, which is twice as big as yours, sold for in 2007 at the height of the real estate bubble.

Conservative Valuation Numbers

Lenders aren't stupid. They understand the time it takes to sell second homes in this economy. The same goes for valuing artwork or your wife's jewelry. Putting a value of $100,000 on those objects raises the eyebrows of the banker and regulator.

If you are applying for a loan the first question in their mind is why are you buying toys when the money should go into the business?

And they'll want to know if it's a pattern of extravagance.

And, finally, they'll want to know if those assets are worth what you put down on paper. Are you listing retail or eBay sale values?

If you get hit by a bus, what would your estate value the objects for probate?

We bring back the takeaway from Pawn Stars. Almost everyone who walks in the door has an unrealistic view of what their asset is worth. And the purity of a Pawn Shop setting is that it establishes cash liquidation values.

The seller always has options—they can put it on eBay or they can list it at an auction house. It is not as if the pawn shop is the only game in town. It shows that people's expectations are much higher than true market prices.

Listing on your personal financial statement at a high retail price your grandmother's silver to which you are emotionally attached doesn't make any sense.

Collateral

I love listening to the pundits and commercials that promise easy credit and no liability by forming a corporation. Lenders aren't stupid; if you are working under a corporation, or a partnership, or an LLC, the lender will provide the appropriate paperwork that assures that you are personally responsible for the debt.

Unless you are Warren Buffet or Mark Zuckerberg, you will be asked to provide the personal guaranty. And a personal guaranty is simply that: if the business is unable to meet its obligations, you agree to guaranty and repay the debt from your personal assets or from your spouse's personal income.

And if you take the time to read it, which no one ever does, you will see that the guaranty is backed up by the things you own and the income you will receive in the future.

The only way to break it is to file bankruptcy, and with the changes in the bankruptcy law there are no assurances it will not completely wipe out your liability.

Other documents that the bank will make you sign include a universal commercial code (UCC) filing statement, which is a pink slip against your business assets. It encompasses everything from cash in the bank to accounts receivable, inventory, and equipment. Even your website.

Of course, there are different levels of loans. You may think that the credit card you have is an unsecured line of credit; it is not! You may think that an unsecured loan doesn't have any collateral, but all that means is that the lender must take one additional legal step to seize your assets.

Trust me, based on their experiences of the past several years, they know how to do this very well.

There are various types of "hard money" lenders who will loan you money against your collateral at an exorbitant interest rate.

One of the more ancient loan structures is "factoring." The classic case use of factoring is by garment manufacturers.

It is in the middle of a long hot summer that the manufacturer is sewing winter clothes. Obviously the upfront cost of payroll, electricity, overhead, and raw materials has to be advanced, with the intent to repay after the winter clothes selling season.

Let's assume that the shipment is for Macy's.

Macy's will issue a purchase order for the merchandise they wish to buy, and the classic factoring arrangement is that manufacturer takes the purchase order to a lender and offers Macy's promise to pay as collateral.

A new source of collateral lending—in fact one of the main sources of restaurant financing today—is a loan that is paid back daily from credit card receipts. This type of financing originally started as a hard-money type concept, but lately has garnered more mainstream acceptability.

You need to have a track record, and you need to process your credit card with the lender, which makes the arrangement much more attractive for the lender because they are picking up different types of income streams in their relationship with you.

The basic plan is your agreement to pay a certain percentage of your receivables, or a fixed daily amount, to the lender.

But be prudent; the downside to this type of arrangement is you are giving up future cash income streams for a chunk of cash today. That may make sense if you are running a flower shop in August, where you will operate at a loss until Valentine's Day in February or Mother's Day in May.

Conditions: The One You Don't Have Any Control Over

There are varying definitions of "conditions," one being the conditions the bank will impose on your company. That's how I was taught.

If you are a middle market company, the bank will require you not to go below certain numbers, such as current ratios or cash-to-debt ratios.

The reality for the small business borrower is the sheath of documents you may be required to sign boils down to the simple statement, "We want to be paid. If you don't pay us, you will be sued and forced into bankruptcy. Your life will be ruined and we.....don't......care....."

Others have added "current economic conditions" to this fifth C.

You've heard me rail against business plans, bemoan the failure to account for unintended consequences and condemn spreadsheet-itis sale manipulations, but at the end of the day you must become an expert in your local economy.

The economic viability of where and to whom you sell affects your bottom line.

In Coleman Publishing, as we sell to banks across the country we are directly impacted by the economy nationwide.

Despite operating leaner, meaner and more efficiently, it came as no surprise that our 2009 revenues decreased 33% from 2008. Fortunately we rebounded in 2010 to notch our best year ever.

The Ronald Reagan line of "A rising tide raises all boats" is appropriate. You must account for all economic conditions in your thinking which today are more like a low tide lowers some ships and grounds others.

Every year, I attend the Restaurant Finance & Development Conference sponsored by the *Restaurant Finance Monitor*, a monthly publication providing financial analysis for multiunit restaurants.

The publisher is (and this isn't a joke) John Hamburger.

Anybody who is considering buying or opening a restaurant must attend John's annual Las Vegas conference. He brings together the brightest minds in the restaurant world.

Two years ago, one of the speakers made an amazing statement.

He said that within five years (so now it's within three years) there would be no mom-and-pop casual dining establishments left in the United States. Casual dining is defined as the sit-down restaurants in the niche between coffee shops and upscale steakhouses.

The casual dining arena is the Applebee's, Chili's, Olive Garden niche. The difficulty for the mom-and-pop operator is that they don't have the benchmarks needed to maximize profitability.

They don't have the expertise to compete with the marketing of the national chains. And they don't have the capital to sustain a prolonged economic downturn.

Applebee's operates about 2,000 units nationwide. Their analysts know the benchmarks of the top ten performing units, and why the bottom ten performing units are missing the boat.

They clearly understand all of the deviations of menu pricing schemes, and have cost control to the penny.

They also have a clear understanding of current economic conditions, and how unit locations affect unit profitability.

The successful mom-and-pop operators will have to be different than Applebee's. They will have to offer a different, local experience.

Good luck with that.

Chapter 9:
Franchise vs. Mom-and-Pop Financing

I want to spend some time talking about franchisee financing. I'm a Main Street advocate. And while I lament the increasing homogeny of Main Street with Jack-in-the-Boxes and Subways proliferating across America, these are also Main Street businesses, just ones run by franchisees.

One of the sad fallouts of the British Petroleum oil spill in the Gulf was the consumer avoided BP gas stations, which are independently, American-owned franchises.

The same problem exists for CITGO gas station owners when Mr. Chavez of Venezuela says something stupid and people don't want to support his state's nationalized oil company.

Again it's a negative impact for American business owners.

Up until 2008, franchise financing was attractive to small business lenders. Knowing there was someone behind the borrower—an Old Man holding their hand—sweetened the deal for lenders.

There was a perception that franchise lending was less risky than financing mom-and-pop Main Street.

No longer.

It is a lender's market, and borrowers are no longer in the driver's seat pitting lender against lender to obtain their business.

Today's lenders are more selective. They have created higher standards for the franchise brands they want most. Franchisors, in turn, are required to demonstrate the strength of their brand.

From an underwriting standpoint, performance is key.

It appears franchising will become the new normal for restaurants and the leading franchise sector for SBA financing. By 2013 the majority of restaurants will be part of a chain.

The upscale steak house will be safe. The birthday-and–special-occasion diner should be OK.

But for the average restaurant, what the industry calls the "casual diner," mom-and-pop is in trouble.

The restaurant owner must provide a significantly different experience than one gets at an Applebee's or Denny's.

Independent restaurants are struggling. They have a difficult time competing against chain restaurants.

The franchises have more information to run their business as efficiently as possible. They have marketing power. They are aggressively discounting and marketing those discounts to their target markets.

Lenders prefer franchises and loan approvals are going to experienced managers, specific concepts, and locations where lenders know the area and are comfortable with the brand. The bottom line is that banks want better borrowers.

It is a new decade and lenders are looking closely in their rear view mirrors.

Underwriting the Franchisor

In the good old days of the early 2000s there were almost blanket approvals for franchise concepts. Smaller deals did not require direct experience and larger deals required transferable experience.

An individual with clean credit and cash to inject could obtain financing for a franchise start-up or acquisition.

Large lenders have the resources to perform an extensive analysis of the franchisor just from the data of their own loans.

Community bankers are smarter too. There is much more information available to help them make more informed decisions.

They may obtain risk assessments and benchmark reports from FRANdata, a research information company focused solely on franchising.

They buy Coleman Publishing restaurant loan underwriting guides.

Before the Great Recession, a number of lenders would finance a franchise concept anywhere in the country.

Banking regulators and the lending environment have squashed that.

National lenders (a number of them SBA) who used to finance franchises anywhere in the country have gone the way of the dinosaur.

It is community banks who are filling the gap for franchise lending. And they want some more assurance that the franchisor will be adding more to the deal than simply a name and a cut of the take.

So, without an extensive franchising portfolio to look at and gain perspective, what do community banks look for in a franchise loan application?

First and foremost, the burden of understanding the risk of a franchise system rests squarely with the franchisor.

I know your head is starting to hurt with the similar terms—franchise systems, franchisees and franchisors.

OK, it's time to be cutting edge. The new emerging buzzword for franchisor is "zor".

That's what we'll use to designate the company that is granting you the franchise: McDonald's, Subway, or Sunglass Hut.

Hope it helps.

The zor needs to demonstrate its financial and operational performance.

They have to provide the information for the banker to underwrite the deal.

Here are some of the things that need to be addressed:

Is the franchise on the SBA registry – www.franchiseregistry.com? It's a national registry of franchise brands where the zor applies and has its franchise agreement and documents reviewed at the national level for approval.

-If so, are there any ongoing eligibility issues?

-How many SBA findings are on the registry?

-How long has the zor been in business?

-How many units does the zor have?

-How many of those units have gone bad?

-What is the average loan size?

Not only does the lender want to know how a franchise performs as a whole along with its individual franchise units, but how does it perform relative to others in its peer group?

How does Blimpie compare to the Subway franchise system? This knowledge gives the lender perspective on whether the franchise's performance is outside or within the normal bounds of its peer group.

Lenders should make it clear to the zor that the bank needs to understand the following:

- Financial performance.

- System performance over time.

- Level of support and operational activities provided to franchisees.

- Unit economics.

- A comparison to the competition.

Generally, zors are accepting the responsibility of providing lenders with an in-depth analysis of the franchise.

For community banks that may only underwrite one or two deals for a particular brand, the burden has shifted from the lender doing the research to the zor getting the work done.

The information has always been necessary in order to assess the risk. There has just been a shift in who produces the data.

Franchise vs. Mom-and-Pop

Compared to mom-and-pop shops, at least 60% to 75% of restaurant loan approvals go to franchises. This percentage will increase in the next several years.

There are specific categories of mom-and-pop shops obtaining financing right now—the successful existing restaurant planning to expand or the highly experienced individual who managed a restaurant for someone else and now wants to acquire it.

For all restaurant loans, *performance* is the driver.

There is a general consensus that the franchise business model increases the likelihood of success and decreases the risk when compared to independent restaurants.

But if the zor is not performing, then it does not matter if they are using a franchise business model.

In the early 2000s, during the rising tide of the economy, mistakes could be made at the zor, franchisee, or independent business level, and those mistakes did not prove fatal for the company.

Today we are in an era where the margin for error is less. Because the margin for error is less, performance matters more.

Leading Franchises

The restaurant sector with the fastest growth is "fast-casual" dining, which could be considered fast food on steroids or casual dining restaurants without wait staff.

It is limited service with higher quality food, and it tends to cost a little more than fast food.

The leading franchised restaurant concepts are categorized as fast casual, including Panera Bread, Noodles, and Chipotle Mexican Grill.

But there are troubles.

There are two major issues impacting the restaurant industry right now. The first is that America is in the early stages of a very slow recovery from a brutal consumer recession.

This is hurting all restaurants and their performance is down across the board.

As an example, even through most of 2010, McDonald's was considered bulletproof. Recently it has started showing lower sales numbers.

The second issue is the oversaturation of casual dining restaurants like Applebee's and Chili's, to name a couple. Experts say three to six percent of casual dining restaurants need to close for the sector to restore its equilibrium.

Arguably the biggest beneficiary of the past decade, casual dining restaurants were overbuilt. With increasing bankruptcies and closures, still more need to close before supply equals demand.

We may not see the balance in restaurants restored until 2012.

Conventional lending has largely left the small business lending market. In order to mitigate risk, banks have moved to SBA lending for their small business borrowers.

With higher underwriting standards, more scrutiny of the franchisee and zor has resulted.

These all relate to having a more conservative risk posture than lenders had two or three years ago.

The largest financing gap is in the $2 million to $5 million range. In franchising, these higher dollar loans generally are for a second, third, or fourth business unit.

The increase in the level of SBA lending to $5 million will fill the current gap and have a significant positive impact on franchise lending.

I had heard that one of the biggest opportunities to emerge from the country's recent economic downturn is the mutual incentive for the lending community and the franchising community to work together more closely than ever before.

I wanted to learn more, so I sought out Geoff Seiber of FranFund out of Ft. Worth.

Geoff and his crew match investors with franchise concepts and help ease the transition to becoming a franchisee and a Main Street small business owner.

"There is just a willingness on each side to gather additional information and to work with lenders from the franchise community that was simply not there in the past," said Geoff.

"Not that we didn't want it in the past, but it was much more that they didn't have to before. I think for lenders, there's a major opportunity out there in franchise finance programs. There's almost no competition out there. There are good yields and still we have fair loans, easily scalable and because of what we've been through, there's quite a bit of talent out there available to lenders to help put those packages together."

In the past, zors saw an easy credit philosophy from lenders which was more volume driven.

Geoff explained that there were very few obstacles for a zor's growth plan during this time.

He was on a roll. I just left the recorder on and let him talk:

"The lending side of that equation was just something that they didn't really have to worry about as they were making their projections and their plans for their franchising business—not their operational business, but their actual business of franchising.

"And what has happened is the capital window is shot. As we all know, there was a shrinking pool of qualified applicants because of the underwriting criteria, and the development side of the franchise recruitment side of the zor's business had to change because the people that they had recruited or that might have even been in process at the time were no longer able to qualify for loans.

"So, the credit philosophy shifted first to much more operational, where it still is, and then even more so to the regulatory side. The banks tightened up across the board on what their ability was and what the lenders felt comfortable doing due to some of the regulatory enforcement that was out there.

"There were just a lot of obstacles to growth, which is not good for a zor and his overall business plan.

"Before, zors used to look past any potential issues as long as they received their money. But now, they're concerned about performance because they know if there is an issue it is going to affect their brand.

"This has led to zors taking more time to prepare their franchisees, resulting in a more informed and qualified applicant engaging lenders.

"Zors raised the bar and they needed to. There is absolutely no upside for a zor taking a check if they don't think they can get the unit open. All it does is create problems, hassles, hurt feelings, money going back and forth, and a loss of time, effort, and energy that could have been directed somewhere else.

"Choosing the right zor partners is the key for lenders when planning on entering into franchise lending.

"At FranFund, we call it 'Underwriting the Zor,' and I think it's important to do a few things if you're looking at doing this in any kind of large scale other than just your own community.

"Review the current franchise operations. Know what the unit economics are currently and how they're responding in this environment; you can get that by asking for your financials and your average unit volumes, those sorts of things.

"A lot of that stuff will be in the bank credit report, an industry analysis provided by FRANdata, and that's a good place to get some of that data, but also make sure that the zor's growth plans and commitments are realistic.

"It's nice to say they're going to build all these, but have they taken into effect how they're actually going to pay for that?

"Validating the current franchisees, I think, is one of the easiest and things that could probably be done. You don't have to talk to fifty of them; ten or twelve is a great sampling.

"If you're starting to hear the same thing again and again, you pretty much have it. If you're all over the board, you may want to keep going.

"Happy franchisees pay on time. If you find that the franchisees you're talking to are happy with their business and their decision to be in that industry, and they have an optimistic outlook on what's going on, you're going to find that most often they pay as agreed.

"Review the royalty delinquency reports, and make sure that those aren't increasing. Remember, the first ones not to get paid are the zors and the lender. If you're seeing an upward trend in that, we're probably also going to see an upward trend in loan delinquencies.

"I don't know how to describe the next thing other than as a 'good citizen relationship.' Is the relationship between the zor and the franchisee respective of each other in their roles and are they all good citizens to the entity?

"That's much more a feeling then something you're going to get on paper. But, look at the way that they handle themselves around each other and what you hear them say about each other. When it's there you know it and when it's not, you know it too."

Formerly referred to as the Uniform Franchise Offering Circular (UFOC), the FTD is a place that many initially go to get information on a franchise or zor.

But, this document can be confusing and Geoff warns that some of the information may be diluted because of requirements set by the Federal Trade Commission.

"There's an awful lot of stuff in this document that could be misleading from a lending perspective and just know that it's not intentionally misleading, it's just the way the FTC has set up the requirements for that particular document.

"They didn't set this up as a lender's document, they set it up for themselves.

"And I think that part of the frustration that a zor has for the FTD, is that they would love to put more information in it for the lender, but their limit is involved in both what they can and can't say, as well as what they must and must not say.

"Review the executive team resumes; in the FTDs they're limited as to how much they can say.

"Ask for full blown resumes of that group if you're looking at lending, and make sure that you're getting as much information on the key members of that zor as you are on the borrower himself."

Geoff told me that not every contractual change is necessarily due to a bad loan or a problem. Sometimes it could be a franchisee has been successful enough to decide he can go it alone.

"It's all part of the gathering of information process. You have to dig to get this information, and you can't just skim the surface and jump to conclusions," said Geoff.

"I think that right now it is a neat time as a lender to look at franchise lending. The attitudes of the zors couldn't be more open and wanting to work with the financial community.

"There's easier access to data and easier access to ongoing relationships within the entire franchise industry for those that want to be involved, and the new SBA programs help quite a bit.

"It's a good time for people to be looking at this, and what we do is try to work with a selected group of zors out there to make sure that the lending community gets access to this data in these relationships.

"Franchise concepts are starting to realize that bankers communicate with each other, and that these concepts could be garnering a bad reputation.

"In the past, a lender speaking at a franchise conference was usually delegated to the last day when everyone was ready to go to the airport.

"Now, the lenders tend to be front and center on the first day.

"Everybody wants to know how they can help their franchisees and how they can work within the financial marketplace to make sure their business grows.

"That's a real change that's happened over the last couple of years.

"Lenders are going to continue to be cautious in the future, especially in certain sectors of the industry that have changed more than others.

"The zors can't understand why their numbers are better than ever and yet it's harder than ever for them to get a loan.

"That is just way beyond where their thought processes, but the education process on both sides is helpful here and the more that they understand about your business the easier it is for them to make sure they're giving you the data that they need."

With all this new information available sounds like good news if you want to own a franchise.

Bad news for mom-and-pop.

Chapter 10: Wal-Mart Is the Killer of Main Street

Whether you want to admit it or not, the one absolute takeaway you must remember is if you are opening a Main Street retail store, make sure you have a lot of stuff in it that you can't get in Wal-Mart.

Otherwise you will end up like Circuit City.

Look what happened to one city where the flight of jobs and opening of Wal-Mart killed Main Street.

Downy, California is about fifteen miles south east of downtown LA. It was a farming community until the post-World War II industrial boom turned it into a manufacturing city.

Downey used to house Boeing's North American Aviation Facility that designed and built the Apollo lunar module that landed on the moon.

Along with the city's involvement in the lunar module, Downey became a central hub for airplane and space shuttle manufacturing. In 1999, the Rockwell plant was closed—another California manufacturing facility lost.

Those well-paying middle-class jobs are long gone from California.

As an aside, did you know that at one time California had fourteen automobile factory plants? Guess how many operate in the Golden State today? Not a single one. Those middle-class jobs are gone too.

Today, Downey's Main Street is decimated.

Appliance stores, office supply stores, furniture stores, movie theaters, hardware stores, mom-and-pop restaurants, and auto parts stores have all been replaced with PayDay Cash Advance shops, liquor stores, and pawn shops.

The death of Downey's Main Street? Loss of middle class jobs, sure. But more importantly, Wal-Mart.

I have been accused being in the pocket of labor organizations for criticizing Wal-Mart. Not true. My opposition to Wal-Mart has to do with its role in the death of Main Street. Not for its labor policies.

For moving in and seducing local politicians and a community with the fairy tale that big box national impersonal centers are better than a tree-lined Main Street run by mom-and-pop.

Mom-and-pop shops define a community's character, retain dollars locally, give the high school kids their first job, sponsor the July 4th barbecue, and create an environment of a town's worth.

Oh yeah, all the while looking out that the streets are safe from crime and ensuring steady increases in home property values.

I am not discussing whether Wal-Mart is good or bad for the American economy.

I support their right to run their shop any way they choose. Obviously America, and now the world, votes with its pocketbook and says it supports Wal-Mart's business model.

I am simply pointing out the fact that we have transitioned from a 1950's idyllic Main Street to an urban sprawling sameness of large, grey, national retail chains.

You could go to any shopping center in America and you wouldn't be able to figure out which part of the country you are in.

The U.S. Small Business Administration hosts an annual Small Business Week. The purpose of the week is to triumph small business, anoint winners from each state, and promote the economic benefits of a robust American small business community.

Good stuff to promote Main Street.

But guess who SBA has as the main sponsor?

Unbelievably, it's Sam's Club, a division of Wal-Mart.

Wal-Mart pays a hefty fee to the SBA for this honor. Wal-Mart's reasoning? They want to have the small businesses that are left to buy their products from them.

Items like office supplies that used to be sold by the local stationery store, ladders and light bulbs that used to be sold by the local hardware store, desks that used to be sold by the local furniture store, cleaning supplies that used to be sold by local janitorial services....well, you get the picture.

SBA's reasoning? I guess they want the check from Wal-Mart. SBA certainly isn't concerned about aligning itself with an entity that has contributed to an epidemic of small business failures.

I guess the fee paid by Wal-Mart offsets some of the losses incurred by the government and banks for businesses put out of business by Wal-Mart.

Small business is unorganized on a national level; they are too busy keeping their head above water to worry about keeping up with national trends. But the seediness of Wal-Mart's organization on America has been devastating when you drive up and down the local Main Streets of the country.

In Downey, California, three Wal-Marts surround the city: Paramount, Norwalk, and Pico Rivera City. Downey's Main Street jobs have been replaced by Wal-Mart's employees.

I certainly understand the attractiveness of Wal-Mart; they have done a masterful job of *branding* themselves as a low-price discounter.

But when you look at their *financials*, they certainly are not. There is a price to be paid for standing in long lines, walking ten minutes from the parking lot to the door, and going through a TSA-type security search of your receipt and cart when you exit the store after checkout.

I guess they presume you are a guilty of shoplifting and you must provide a receipt to prove your innocence.

For Downey, this was particularly insidious because all three stores that ring the city do not contribute any sales tax dollars to the city's coffers.

I'm not advocating a Pollyannaish solution, that you only seek out small businesses to cater to and to ignore the large super centers.

I understand the decision making process of foregoing your neighbor Ace Hardware store and driving the extra thirty minutes to Home Depot for the larger selection.

I understand the advantage of being able to buy a bag of diapers at 3:00 am, although thank God I don't fit that demographic anymore.

I simply bring up this point to illustrate—and this is the key point of the chapter—the difficulties the small business owner must concern themselves with in competing in a free market.

They must offer the customer a unique experience and breadth of products that they can't get at Wal-Mart. Or online at Amazon.com.

I choose not to shop at Wal-Mart and avoid the super centers as much as possible because I understand the trade-off of the everything-under-one-roof versus a good customer experience on Main Street.

But there are limits.

For example, do I continue to deal with my local pharmacist when they close at 1:00 pm on Saturday and are closed on Sunday, when I can get the product at a Wal-Mart pharmacy on a 24/7 basis?

I know that Wal-Mart or a large chain such as CVS or Rite-Aid will have an app for my iPad or iPhone to manage my meds a lot more conveniently than the local guy. Do I sacrifice personal service just because Wal-Mart is open on Sunday?

The cost is the same. So that's not a factor.

Do I want to trade the service of being treated respectfully and the clerk knowing who I am for 24-hour convenience and a faceless clerk who doesn't know me?

Sadly, America continues to vote for convenience over service.

I am not completely anti-big business.

Consider the airline industry: Would you feel more comfortable flying an airline with a couple of planes or a major carrier that has standardized safety protocol in place?

No argument from me there.

I am simply saying there is a trade-off. The small business owner cannot provide the wide range of products, but they can choose to differentiate themselves in a way that Wal-Mart cannot.

Unfortunately, the small business owner, and probably most Americans, doesn't understand the current state of technology and the dramatic impact it has on their lives. Small business owners must become experts in this area to survive. Their competitors have.

When I asked my pharmacist where he was in developing an app, he looked at me as if I needed some different type of meds.

I tried for a compromise. How about if I email you when I run out? Sure, he said, but be sure to call us and tell us when you do that. We don't check the email that often.

Sigh.

My favorite Mexican restaurant in town is struggling because a Chipotle has opened.

Here's a story that illustrates why.

I was heading out to the bank when my son asked me asked if I could drop him off to grab his lunch. He said it would just take a second. Sure, no problem.

We drive up to the Chipotle and he jumps out. I circle around to find a parking spot when I see him waving me down. He had been out of the car less than a minute.

That's odd.

"What happened?" I asked.

"Nothing," he said.

I notice he's got a Chipotle bag in his hand.

Now I'm really confused.

"I don't understand. How did that go so fast? You were in and out in thirty seconds."

I glance over my shoulder to see if by some strange reason the kid had decided to turn rouge and rob the place. I want to see if he's being chased by security flying out the door after him. Which immediately makes me his accomplice, as the getaway driver.

I think he says, "Yep, they're really fast," but it was hard to figure out if those were his exact words because he's stuffing his mouth with big bites of burrito.

I pull the car over.

I grab the bag and look in it. No wads of stolen bills, that's a good sign. Inside is a receipt. And the strangest thing of all, his name is on the outside of the bag.

Ahhh. I'm not completely stupid. Must have been a phone order.

But how did he pay for it so fast? There was a line of people at the counter when he jumped out of the car!

"Did you pay for this?" I ask.

He sighed, "Of course."

He put his burrito down and between gulps of air explained to his addled, feeble-minded old man what happened.

"Look here," he says showing me his iPhone. "This is an app for Chipotle. You check off what you want in your burrito, the type of cheese, hot or mild salsa, onions, whatever. You give them your name and what time you'll pick it up. You go in, there's a bag with you name on it, you grab it and it's lunch time."

He went back to chomping on what was left of the burrito.

"That's pretty cool," I said, "but how do you pay for it?

He gave me the look of one who knows it all and is dealing with someone headed to the retirement home soon and sighed, "They have mom's credit card on file."

To survive, small businesses must learn to compete with this type of service.

Back to Wal-Mart.

Another reason I dislike Wal-Mart is that their relationship with its vendors is exploitative. First, it pays its vendors in a 90 to 120-day cycle, forcing the vendor to be its bank.

They even brag in their financials that they have negative working capital, e.g., they owe more money in the next twelve months than they have from a combination of cash in the bank and inventory on the shelves.

Wal-Mart would claim that the arrangement works because of their advanced inventory control systems that limit the amount of inventory they need to keep on the shelves.

I would agree with that. Another reason why it's difficult for Main Street to compete.

But stretching out payment to vendors—effectively borrowing at a zero interest rate from them—clearly establishes who the Old Man is in that relationship.

My own experience as a Wal-Mart vendor was many years ago, when I produced a videotape with San Diego Padre player Tony Gwynn.

We sold a number of tapes to Wal-Mart in exchange for a personal appearance by Tony Gwynn. Not only did Wal-Mart not pay us for ninety days, but after ninety days the unsold tapes were shipped back to our warehouse.

When I complained, they basically said, "We.....don't.....care. Sue us. You're lucky we sent you back your tapes."

Vendors don't really sell to Wal-Mart as much as they *consign* inventory to them. Wal-Mart is notorious for negotiating the lowest possible price without regard to quality.

Back in the day, when I did shop at Wal-Mart, my wife and I found a room air-conditioning unit at an unbelievable $199 price.

You get what you pay for. The air-conditioning unit barely lasted a year.

Wal-Mart's abuse of its small business vendors is legendary, and once Wal-Mart takes the lion's share of a small business's revenues, the small business owner becomes an employee of Wal-Mart. Not even that; it's more like a temporary worker or a freelance contractor.

Wal-Mart continually renegotiates to lower the price of a product and is notorious for dropping vendors.

If a small business has a significant portion of its production tied to Wal-Mart and it loses its Wal-Mart contract, it is almost impossible for them to find new retailers and keep their doors open.

And this is the main sponsor of SBA's Small Business Week?

Chapter 11:
The Commercial Real Estate Bubble

Let me explain the commercial real estate bubble, and how it is affecting Main Street.

The example I want to use is a flower shop in Simi Valley, California.

Earlier in the book I talked about how I met Michael Mutal and financed his flower shop business, Michael's Flowers.

Running a flower shop is a very difficult business; the owner receives his or her profits at very select times of the year: Valentine's Day, Mother's Day, the senior prom, etc. The rest of the year they are lucky to break even.

The number of weddings and funerals in a month determines the shop's profitability.

The economy has forced all Americans to cut back on their spending, and unfortunately for flower shop owners, flower purchases are considered an affordable luxury.

In 2007, battered by declining revenues, Mike went through his options and realized that as long as the operation was still profitable, he considered his finances in order because the store property was worth a million dollars—property he will inherit one day.

His property is on a corner lot and has four storefronts. The flower shop is the main tenant, taking about half the space, leaving the other half for lease.

At that time, Mike was receiving rent from the three spaces next to the flower shop leased out at $1,500, $1,000 and $1,000, to a contractor, a real estate agent, and an income tax professional respectively.

With the rent he paid to himself of $4,000, the total income of the property was $7,500 a month.

Commercial real estate is different from residential real estate.

The value of residential real estate is based on comparisons. If your neighbor sells his house for $500,000 and you have the identical house in a similar neighborhood, then the market views your house as being valued at $500,000.

Commercial real estate however, is not valued by this method. Rather, it is based upon the income produced by the space, which actually makes a lot more sense than housing valuations.

If you are a borrower and you go to the bank with a piece of raw land, most bankers will not value that property. If you think your piece of property is worth x-amount of dollars, your valuation is faulty.

Raw land is only worth what someone down the road will pay for it. It doesn't produce income; it produces only expenses in the form of property taxes, maintenance, and liability insurance.

Now back to Mike. In 2007, he was collecting $7,500 monthly in rent. And we know that the value of the property is determined by the future income stream of rents.

In order to calculate that value, you must use an interest rate, what is known as a "cap rate."

A cap rate is the amount of money a reasonable investor would expect as a return for their investment. In 2007, a six percent return was considered reasonable.

Six percent is a low number, but remember the times: cheap money flowed like water, the prime rate was down and investors were easily able to borrow money at low rates and receive investments in a variety of different financial options, including commercial real estate.

When you crunch the numbers, a $7,500 monthly income at a six percent cap rate puts you at a million dollar value.

This analysis holds true whether it's a retail shop, a warehouse, a storage facility, or a sports facility; all commercial real estate values are based upon cash flow.

What happened in 2010?

As we've mentioned, even in the best of times running a flower shop is a difficult proposition, and the recession has done nothing but exacerbate those financial problems.

Reduced revenue caused our friend Mike to reduce expenses: staffing, purchases, and most importantly, his rental payment. In 2010 he told his dad he had to reduce his rent from $4,000 to $2,500 a month.

One of the tenants, in a similar financial situation, reduced their rent payment from $1,500 to $1,000.

The other two tenants eventually stopped paying rent and moved out, leaving Mike's monthly rent income at $3,500.

The declines were across the board. Small business owners all have seen the decline in their stock market portfolios, the decline in the value of their homes, and the decline in the value of their businesses.

Declines in values have also extended to those who own commercial real estate.

Here's why.

The lease income on the property declined from $7,500 a month to $3,500 a month.

That's a little over 50% of the revenue generated by the property,

So is it safe to assume the value of the property dropped in half, to $500,000?

Not so fast.

Here's why.

With credit and investment opportunities severely constricted, those with cash now require a higher rate of return on investment. It is a simple supply-and-demand analysis.

Where investors were likely to accept a six percent cap rate in 2007, by 2010 they wanted a cap rate at ten percent.

A higher cap rate reduces the value of the property. So, with this new calculation, our once million-dollar property is now only worth $360,000 today.

Now Mike is fortunate that his Dad owns the property free and clear so Mike is fine, even though our friendship has taken a hit since I'm the one who's explained to him he is no longer a paper millionaire!

But what about someone else?

Let's talk about a hypothetical situation for Sam.

Assume that in 2007 Sam bought his commercial real estate property on Main Street for his business for $1 million.

It doesn't matter what type of property it is—whether it's a warehouse, office building or a specialty piece of property like a restaurant.

But for our example, let's make Sam the town veterinarian who has a bought a standard piece of property on Main Street.

Standard financing in 2007 was 75%.

Being a good businessman, Sam put down the $250,000 cash he had saved over the years and got a loan of $750,000 loan against a million-dollar piece of property.

We made the numbers similar to the flower shop example, so let's say Sam was charging his business $7,500 a month rent for the property.

For tax reasons Sam bought the property in his name, not in the name of the business.

Unlike most residential real estate loans, commercial real estate loans have a maturity of five to ten years out.

Therefore, Sam's five-year-old commercial real estate loan comes due in 2012.

Sam is no different than any other small businessman in the country. The recession has affected him. He didn't lose any money in 2010, but he didn't make any either. Sales are down.

With ten percent unemployment in his town and twenty percent underemployment, folks just can't afford to take care of their pets the way they would like.

But he's made all his payments on time—the car, perhaps an equipment lease, and of course the building.

He's never missed a payment.

Unfortunately, his credit score has *worsened.*

Here's why.

Sam had a $10,000 line of credit with Advanta, the small business specialty credit card company that went bankrupt. With $6 billion in credit lines, Advanta alone accounted for over five percent of lost credit card lines during the Great Recession.

Advanta tried to mitigate its risk by charging a steep interest rate—in Sam's case it was 36%.

Sam, being prudent, simply paid off the balance each month.

As an aside, that was the problem with Advanta's model. It priced itself so high its better credit-worthy customers avoided borrowing money from Advanta and simply used the card for monthly expenses.

That left Advanta with a pool of customers who needed credit, regardless of the cost.

Prior to Advanta's bankruptcy filing, the company's first step was to freeze all of its credit lines.

Along with everyone else, Sam got a notice that his line of credit was canceled. While bemoaning the loss of the credit line, he wasn't too worried. He only owed $600 and paid it off in full the following month, as he did every month.

The problem is that Sam's *credit score* took a hit. Instead of showing a $10,000 credit line and owing $600, Advanta now reported Sam was at the top of his credit line, owing 100% of the credit line amount.

He owed $600 on a $600 line.

The second hit occurred when Advanta reported to Sam's credit agencies that it canceled his credit line.

More hits came to Sam's credit. He had a home equity line of credit he never used. The lender canceled it due to declining home values in his area. Sam's availability of credit was drying up, causing a decline in his credit scores.

Those were minor annoyances for Sam. His real problems will occur in 2012, and the sad part Sam probably doesn't even know it yet.

He will walk into his bank expecting to simply roll over the note. After all, he's never been delinquent and even made a couple of thousand dollars in a down year last year.

He's paid down the loan to $700,000.

The bank will order an appraisal.

Well, the appraiser, who after seeing his brethren's run of the business with lawsuits and disgruntled bank clients, and knowing it's the bank who pays his bills, not the borrower, and who has been told by the bank to be conservative, conservative, conservative, will do just that.

Now hold on, I can hear your screaming.

You're saying that I just wrote that commercial real estate is different than residential real estate and that it is not dependent on comparables, it's dependent on cash flow.

Ahh, remember that number, the cap rate. The appraiser isn't going to use an old 2007 six percent number. He'll double it—to twelve percent.

The value of Sam's property has now plummeted in half, to $500,000.

But he owes $700,000. He's underwater.

That is the core of the impending commercial real estate bubble.

If the bank extends the loan at $700,000, the underlying property is only "worth" $500,000, before liquidating and holding expenses.

The regulators will demand the bank write off a significant portion of the loan. No bank will do that. Renew a loan and take a $250,000 loss at booking?

The bank will demand Sam come up with $250,000 cash as it refinances the note at 90% of it's $500,000 appraisal.

Sam doesn't have the cash. And his credit score has fallen. And his cash flow is historically "negative" by definition.

The regulators and market forces will demand the bank foreclose on Sam. *Even though he never missed a payment.*

And probably sell the building at auction for 50% of its appraised value, or $250,000, further depressing values.

Welcome to the commercial real estate bubble of 2011 and 2012.

Chapter 12: Greed, Lies, and the Banker Who Got Caught

In 2008 Business Loan Express (BLX), the nation's second largest SBA lender, closed its doors and filed for bankruptcy.

We expect a local restaurant to file for bankruptcy, but not a national small business lender making $500 million of loans a year, with over $4 billion in loans on its books.

The biggest scandal in the history of small business lending, the BLX bankruptcy rocked the small business lending community.

Of course, in the news this bankruptcy was soon overshadowed by the failure of much larger financial institutions, Lehman Brothers, Bear Stearns, Washington Mutual, Wachovia, and Indy-Mac, just to name a few.

Hundreds of BLX employees lost their jobs. Thousands of others who relied on BLX's loans received pink slips.

What happened?

Greed. Old fashioned greed.

I've talked about how a bank makes a profit by taking money, turning it into inventory, and selling loans to Main Street.

It's not a bad model. Borrow money at the Fed ATM window at 1/2 percent and lend it out at eight percent. The interest rate spread covers a lot of nice office space, good salaries, company expense accounts and credit cards, not to mention the ability to travel from time to time on the company dime.

Oh yeah, there needs to be something left over to buy Coleman Publishing's newsletter and loan underwriting guides!

Anyway, the U.S. Small Business Administration has received its share of criticism over the years. Its response to providing 9/11 loans to small business was bungled.

Also charged with providing disaster relief to home owners, the agency became the poster child of governmental incompetence with its handling of Hurricane Katrina victim loan applications.

Fortunately for Main Street, it has done more good than harm, as evidenced by the $250 billion of loans Main Street would not have received without SBA.

Now it's true, some of those loans go bad—we've referenced the 20% failure rate since 2000.

But look behind the numbers. The loss rate is actually two percent a year, a very reasonable number.

In fact, the dirty little secret the agency's detractors won't tell you is for its major loan programs, 7(a) and 504, the fees paid by the borrowers *exceed* the program's losses.

Until the Great Recession, SBA's lending programs made money for the government. What other federal government program can make that claim?

In that sense it is an excellent example how a public-private partnership should work. The private sector—the bank—provides the money and lending expertise, and SBA provides the federal government guaranty and oversight of the program.

How SBA began is an interesting story.

Growing up in Abilene, Kansas at the turn of the twentieth century, General Dwight David Eisenhower was truly a Main Street boy.

We all remember the warning he made when he left office after two terms as president of the United States to be aware of the military-industrial complex.

His concerns about the overreach of large corporations developed long before that day.

He was always a supporter of the unique problems of running a Main Street small business.

During World War II he was instrumental in starting the Small War Plants Corporation (SWPC), whose job it was to ensure small business got an appropriate piece of military supply contracts.

The military bought an enormous amount of material that could be supplied by Main Street manufacturers including food, clothing, ammunition, and office supplies.

Small business could produce key components for ships, airplanes, and trucks on a subcontract basis for big companies like Boeing, Lockheed, Kaiser Shipbuilding, and General Motors.

SWPC would also help Main Street with these contracts by providing federal government financing to buy the raw materials, meet the payroll, and pay the rent and electric bills.

After Eisenhower was elected president he believed small business needed a champion, a mentor who would help them against the onslaught of corporate lobbyists and special interests.

In 1953, with President Eisenhower's support, SBA was born.

Over fifty years later, for every BLX scandal there are thousands of success stories.

Guess what these companies have in common: Federal Express, Intel, and Tom's of Maine?

All received SBA financing.

Not everyone can be a gazelle, but the majority of SBA loan borrowers have been good citizens, paying taxes, hiring people, and giving back to the community.

Most small business bankers I talk with share Eisenhower's passion for Main Street.

Sure, they are in corporate America wearing a suit and tie, but they have found a rewarding career helping those who create jobs and who create value in their local communities.

Except a guy named Patrick Harrington. His passion was money. Not for Main Street—for himself.

Harrington was the BLX executive vice president based out of a suburb of Detroit.

His greed got him convicted for committing the largest small business loan fraud in history—over $85 million.

Today, he has a cot for ten years in a federal minimum-security prison in Kentucky, a Madoff-lite sentence.

Bank fraud affects everyone. It stains the other 99.99% of honest bankers.

It gives the SBA program a black eye and gives ammunition to its critics.

And it usually ensnares small business operators who don't think the adage of "if it's too good to be true, it is" doesn't apply to bankers and their banks.

What happened?

I've gone through the discourse that a bank's inventory is money.

Well, just like any other business, the bank only makes a profit when it sells inventory. And like other businesses it will compensate its salesmen when they sell inventory.

Harrington made over $4 million in five years selling loans for BLX.

And while Harrington was crooked, there was also a flaw in BLX's model: Harrington was able to *approve* the same loans for which he was then paid a sales commission.

He wasn't interested in making good small business loans. He was only interested in making commissions off of deals. Eighty percent of the loans he approved defaulted.

As with any other manufacturing process, a loan is comprised of hundreds of components—in this case, pieces of paper.

And like other manufacturing processes there are checklists. Start at the top and work your way through the end and the bank has manufactured inventory—a loan.

Harrington was a checklist banker.

The checklist calls for reams of tree-killing paper: three years of business financial statements, three years of tax returns, the current balance sheet, the current profit and loss statement, accounts receivable and aging accounts payable, business licenses, business valuations, business appraisals, equipment lists, detailed lists of where the loan money is going, copies of bank statements, detailed explanation of where cash down payments come from, three years tax returns of all owners, along with their financial statements.

And I haven't even listed the long list of forms the bank makes everyone sign.

It is a complicated and convoluted process.

Assemble everything on the checklist and you have a loan.

Harrington was fast and loose with the rules. He cut corners putting inventory on the floor.

What was his crime?

He was convicted of the simplest white-collar crimes; lying to the government and to the SBA, and then covering it up.

Harrington found out that there isn't much of a defense to lying to a grand jury about a cover-up.

As with most federal programs, SBA lending rules are governed by thousands of pages of regulations.

At the time, SBA had very extensive verbiage on its definition of a small business. Who was eligible for small business financing alone counted for hundreds of pages of SBA regs.

The SBA/bank public private partnership has evolved over the years. At one time SBA approved all loans funded by banks.

That was inefficient. Bankers approve loans all the time. That's what they do.

So the relationship changed. Banks would be in charge of what they know best—making and approving loans.

And SBA assumed a role of what it does best—providing incentives to banks to get capital to Main Street at the lowest possible cost to the taxpayer. Part of this mandate is to audit the banks to make sure they are following SBA's regulations.

And SBA has the hammer. While the bank has the ability to approve and fund a loan with a federal government loan guaranty, the bank must follow SBA's rules.

If the bank doesn't follow the rules and SBA's regulations, the remedy is simple. SBA won't pay the bank its loan guaranty for loan losses.

Seems a fair trade-off for Main Street, the bank, and the taxpayer.

Back to Harrington.

When Harrington approved a loan he faxed a piece of paper to SBA asking for a federal government guaranty, usually 75% of the loan.

SBA issued a document formalizing the guaranty and giving the bank a loan number.

That's it. Pretty simple stuff.

However, when the bank faxes the loan guaranty request, an officer of the bank must sign it.

The signing officer certifies to SBA the loan is being made according to SBA's rules and regulations, and, this is the important part, the business is eligible for a guaranty.

Patrick Harrington—the same guy who was originating the loans—signed hundreds of these certifications for BLX.

At least seventy-six times, he knew the loans weren't eligible.

The U.S. Attorney who brought the charges against Harrington made the case simple.

By signing and faxing the documents, he said Harrington was lying to the federal government and committing wire fraud.

Harrington had no defense. With secretly recorded FBI tapes of him boasting about his grand jury cover-up, the case never went to trial. He pled guilty and took his ten years.

But it was a great ride for Harrington while it lasted.

In 2002 and 2003 he personally made over $1 million each year. His base salary was an eye-popping $400,000.

BLX paid him annual retention bonuses of $150,000 during the last three years of his employment.

He turned BLX into his personal ATM. In 2002 he made over $500,000 alone in commissions on loans he approved.

Here's how the fraud worked.

The epicenter was the small businesses in Detroit and its surrounding environs owned by citizens and immigrants of middle eastern descent.

The businesses were meat-and-potatoes operations, those that provide services used by their customers every day—motels, gas stations, convenience stores, and restaurants.

While Harrington had the ability to approve his own deals he couldn't control everything. Since he was the only one indicted, the conspiracy consisted of fooling others at BLX.

And that's a long list.

At a minimum he had to fool at least three people within BLX. (He tried to mitigate his prison time and claimed others at BLX were involved, but the U.S. attorney has never brought charges against other BLX employees.)

The BLX credit underwriter would be responsible for putting together the package documenting the bank's approval of the loan.

They would sign off on real estate and business appraisals. They would check with the IRS to make sure the tax returns provided by the borrower were the same as the ones filed with the IRS.

They would verify the equity injection.

Ah—the equity injection. The layman's term is "down payment." SBA and the bank call it equity injection.

This is the key part of Harrington's fraud and the need to build a network of co-conspirators.

SBA, and the bank for that matter, requires a borrower to have some skin in the game when they start a business or buy real estate.

Demonstrating equity injection is the trickiest part of the fraud. The other parts of the conspiracy were easy to put together by Harrington.

There would be a real estate broker who wanted to move property and make their commissions. That was simple.

Next would be a loan broker who put the players together.

Brokers only get paid when deals get done, so he only had to find a couple of crooked ones who were greedy like him.

Next they needed a patsy, someone to sign all the documents—a straw buyer.

They would recruit someone from Detroit's middle-eastern ethnic community who had adequate credit, and have them sign all the loan documents and then walk away from the deal.

They would be paid a fee out of the loan proceeds for their services.

That's four so far in the conspiracy.

The fifth was a little more difficult to find.

They needed another banker. Someone who would vouch that the straw man was legitimate and held a couple of hundred thousand dollars in a bank account.

Enter Deborah Lazenby, an assistant vice president of The Huntington National Bank.

Not only would she sign papers saying there was money on deposit, she went so far as to issue fake cashier's checks drawn on The Huntington National Bank.

She got two years in jail and was slapped with $4 million in restitution. But I'm getting off the track of the story.

The last person Harrington had to fool within BLX would be the loan closer.

This person would take all the papers submitted by the borrower, take the credit memorandum composed by the credit underwriter, gather all the outside reports, appraisals, credit reports, environmental reports, buy/sell agreements, and escrow statements, and make a loan file.

Then the loan closer prepares all the loan documents, which is the last step in the bank's inventory creation process.

The loan closer gets signatures from everyone.

And verifies equity injection. And gets the cash.

In this fraud, Deborah Lazenby would send over the fake cashier's check.

Technically it wasn't a fake. She was authorized to sign the cashier's check. And when she affixed her signature the check became legit.

The problem for The Huntington National Bank was there was nothing to back up the check. *That* was fraud. They were "out of balance" to use a banker's phrase.

It was in their "suspense" account.

With the bogus cashier's check in place, the loan closer would bundle everything up and send the completed loan file—the new inventory of the bank—to the closing attorney or title company.

The attorney would check everything over and disburse the loan.

To tidy everything up, the very next day Lazenby's fake cashier's check would be covered by loan proceeds.

Here's a typical transaction.

One of the brokers would identify a gas station for sale. For purposes of the hypothetical, the seller is asking $700,000.

The broker, who cannot obtain an SBA loan himself because of a criminal record, enlists the assistance of a neighbor or relative who agrees to assist the broker by putting the gas station in his or her name.

The broker assures the straw purchaser that he or she will not have to put anything into the deal, and will receive a percentage of the proceeds when the station is subsequently sold and, perhaps, even a percentage of its profits.

The broker then fills out all of the necessary paperwork to obtain the loan, including false employment histories, false financial statements, and false evidence of an "equity injection."

In order to qualify for an SBA guaranteed loan, the borrower must inject their own assets into the business, typically 20% of the purchase price. All of the BLX loans investigated revealed false equity injections.

Because the loan will not include an equity injection, and because the broker is desperate for funds to cover another failing business, the broker increases the sales price to cover the missing equity injection and to assure excess funds at closing

In this hypothetical, therefore, the broker inflates the sale price to $1,000,000.

Harrington would then take the fraudulent paperwork and approve of the loan.

The final step in the transaction is the closing and disbursement of funds.

At least one title company employee was recruited into the conspiracy to facilitate closings.

The closing documents would reflect that an equity injection was paid at, or prior to, the closing.

A copy of a cashier's check would be accepted, instead of an original.

Parties not involved in the purchase (but who were involved in the conspiracy) attend the loan closing.

At the closing, one would expect funds to be distributed according to a preapproved settlement statement. However, at this hypothetical closing, funds are disbursed to various parties not associated with the transaction.

Individuals involved in Harrington's conspiracy profited in many ways. For the brokers, excess funds were disbursed at closings that paid off everyone involved.

Harrington, who was under pressure at BLX to produce loans, received his sales commission for creating inventory for the bank.

His judge summed it up succinctly at his sentencing: "Harrington was involved in a conspiracy of several people who over-appraised property; flipped property; recruited straw buyers; made false statements on the loan applications; prepared false documents; submitted false equity injection documents; and conducted illegal disbursement of funds at closings.

"Those persons involved in recruiting the straw buyers, appraising property, closing the loans and processing loan applications all financially benefited. The only ones who generally did not financially benefit were the legitimate sellers, who signed closing documents that did not accurately reflect the sales' terms, and the straw purchasers, who sometimes even lost their personal homes to BLX liens when 'their' loans defaulted.

"When the value of the property is inflated, the amount of the loan often exceeds the real value of the business, creating a situation where the average daily sales cannot generate enough proceeds to cover the loan payment, let alone generate any profit. Inherent in the criminal scheme is a recipe for failure."

Whenever I give a speech to bankers I usually include the wording of the bank's request for a guaranty from the SBA.

The wording is pretty simple: "I approve this application to SBA subject to the terms and conditions outlined above. Without the participation of SBA, to the extent applied for, we would not be willing to make this loan, and in our opinion the financial assistance applied for is not otherwise available on reasonable terms.

"I certify that none of the Lender's employees, officers, directors, or substantial stockholders (more than 10%) has a financial interest in the applicant.

"I approve and certify that the applicant is a small business according to the standards in 13 CFR 121, the loans proceeds will be used for an eligible purpose, and the owners and managers of the business are of good character."

The problem is most bankers who sign the document never consider the implications of their signature.

Consider this analogy.

Let's say a Mr. Adams is a wanna-be Main Street entrepreneur businessman who has a brilliant idea that American wedding couples want to go old school and have a plastic groom and bride in the image of Prince William in a tux and Kate Middleton in her white wedding dress for their wedding cake.

Adams convinces a Chinese company to manufacturer and ship over 100,000 plastic statues at $1 each.

To induce the Chinese to ship without any upfront cash, he tells them he has a purchase order from Wal-Mart that says they'll buy them for $2 apiece.

That's a cool hundred grand, which he promises to split with the Chinese.

Two problems. Wal-Mart doesn't share his optimism and their order never materializes. He over-promises and can't deliver.

Adams has misjudged the market. He can't close with Wal-Mart. There's no action on eBay. The Pawn Stars laugh him all the way back to the state line.

No one wants the William and Kate figurines.

Of course the Chinese want their money, so after a while they sue him.

Mr. Adams has his day in court, and he's ordered to pay the Chinese the hundred grand.

He sadly realizes he won't be the next Mr. Zuckerberg and he becomes a Main Street casualty, filing bankruptcy.

Not a happy ending to a failed business partnership. But no laws were broken.

They each take their losses and move on, a little sadder and wiser from their failed partnership.

It's a different story when you go into partnership with the federal government who owns prisons and employs a lot of people who carry guns.

If something goes wrong, they won't buy you a nice sendoff dinner and take care of your wife and family the way the mob does. The feds will bring everything they have against you.

In Harrington's case it was the FBI, IRS, ICE, Secret Service. Even SBA! Did you know SBA has its own agents who carry guns? They do!

The FBI wiretapped him.

Picture this.

It's around Christmas. Harrington is having a nice little dinner party at his house. There is a knock on the door.

It's a couple of FBI agents in their FBI stenciled jackets.

They turn on a hand-held tape recorder.

Harrington hears himself talking to one of his loan broker co-conspirators, who had flipped and was wearing a wire.

It's not pretty. They play the tape where Harrington hears himself telling the broker to lie to the FBI where the equity injection is coming from.

"Just call it f—ing mattress money," says Harrington. "Say it was cash that had been saved over the years."

Oops, that's witness tampering.

Then the kicker.

Money, Money Everywhere - 162

Check out the master of the universe's quotes. He's in control. The problem is Harrington is being wiretapped in a conversation with a loan broker named Imad Deaibes.

Harrington: Okay, I got to get a new car. You still driving that BMW?

Deaibes: Yea.

Harrington: You got to get rid of that thing man.

Deaibes: Why?

Harrington: Makes you a target. These f—ing guys see you driving around in that thing and they want to hang your ass. Why don't you downscale a little bit?

Deaibes: I am.

Harrington: One of the problems is these government guys get on your ass and they're making forty-five grand a year. Killing themselves with two kids and they see you touring around in a f—ing BMW.

Game. Set. Match.

Being a crook is one thing, but being an arrogant SOB will make the landing a little bit harder.

Back to the certifications that bankers sign for SBA. I don't want them waking up at 2:00 a.m. worrying about everything they have ever said to SBA.

The feds aren't going to come after them for petty paperwork problems.

But if there is a problem, that's where they will nail you.

And never forget. SBA is part of the federal government. It's a crime to lie to SBA.

SBA borrower fraud is as glamorous for a U.S. attorney as being able to nail a white-collar banker, but this is how borrowers get nailed.

Somewhere buried in all your SBA loan paperwork is an IRS Form 4506.

Once you sign it you give the bank the ability to obtain a copy of your federal income tax returns directly from the IRS. Some banks make you sign this in blank, so they can get copies of your future tax returns, even if you don't want the bank to see them.

It's a fairly automated process and the bank usually gets the information within a couple of weeks.

The bank will compare the information it receives from the IRS with your tax returns. If they don't match, and if you've submitted a different set of returns to the bank than to the IRS, there is no defense. I've never seen one of those cases go to trial. Rather than risk twenty years in prison, they all plead out.

Next time you read about some poor sap caught up in the mortgage fraud mess check out what they are being convicted of.

Not receiving money for a house they couldn't afford, not for failing to pay the mortgage; they are convicted of lying to the bank about their income.

Chapter 13: The Three F's -Friends, Family, or Fools

I've explained bank-think, and I know the small business owners reading this book are getting anxious.

Enough with the history—what does one have to do to get a loan today?

Well, it depends on your situation and what bucket the lender will place you into. If your venture is a start-up, you're not going to get a bank loan.

You're going to have to resort to the three F's: Friends, Family, or Fools.

The reality is that it is very difficult to finance a start-up operation from the traditional lending format. Before the Great Recession, it would be perfectly feasible for an employee to retire from Boeing in Seattle, borrow against their 401k, and open up a Subway franchise in El Paso.

And the bank's only concern would be that the borrower had the minimum amount of skin in the game.

Today, those types of scenarios are unable to be financed for a variety of reasons. I've discussed character being the first C.

Today, part of the bank's definition of character is determined by whether the borrower has enough expertise and sufficient local knowledge of the specific global region.

In our example the banker wants to know if that Boeing executive even wants to work in a Subway shop.

The displaced executive must prove they are amiable to their prospective new line of work, familiar with the area, and that they have the emotional fortitude to work in that type of business.

The banker isn't family, they don't want to be your friend, and they certainly don't want to be a fool.

The first piece of advice I would offer to those in the start-up bucket is to treat cash the same way Microsoft, Geico, and smart Main Street operators do: horde it and watch every nickel like a hawk.

Answer this question: "What business do you want to be in?"

Open a restaurant? A new barber shop? A karate studio?

Wrong answers.

You are in the business of collecting cash for your product or service.

The corner printer is not in the printing business, they are not in the conversion-of-paper-and-ink-into-flyers business, or selling printing services; they are in the business of collecting cash from the customer.

I talked earlier about how a small business person would treat $10,000 dollars in cash on their desk, and that it should be treated no differently than a $10,000 paper IOU.

When I started out there was a wanna-be lobbyist from Washington signed up to attend one of my first lending conferences.

The price was around $1,000 for he and his assistant. I had a gut feel it was going to be difficult for me to get paid by this guy.

Before the conference I was calling him every day to let him know I was expecting the money. I explained how I needed the money to prepay the hotel. I went on and on about how important this was and embellished a tad about the impact to my cash flow.

He was the unluckiest man I have ever met.

The bank was always making errors—that's why the credit card numbers he kept giving me never worked. The post office must have had a personal vendetta against him, because it kept losing his mail.

Finally, he committed to bring a check with him when he showed up.

Of course, when he arrived to register for the opening reception he said he didn't have the check and said he would deal with it the next day.

I said no problem. Enjoy yourself. When he showed up the next day without the check I discretely informed him, with a little wild-eyed look in my eye, that I really needed the money, NOW.

He acted all shocked, but it worked. He opened up his wallet, took out a blank check and filled it out. I think his hand was shaking just a little bit.

Fortunately his check didn't bounce.

It wasn't pleasant, but it worked. If I didn't pursue him like he was a man holding ten of my hundred-dollar bills I never would have seen the money.

I'm fortunate in my niche. Bankers are difficult to sell to, but once you close the sale, you almost always get your cash.

I used to say that the telephone company always got paid first, and that may still be true today, though it's probably not the landline but rather the cell phone.

The biggest shock, and it shows my naiveté, was that when I started my business I never realized how many people had their hands out.

Yes, we can complain about government taxes and regulations, but everything must be kept in perspective. I was talking the other day with a fellow publisher who lives in Finland.

We were comparing notes, and I made the usual American complaint about taxes, which made him look at me like I had three heads.

He calmly explained to me that the tax rate in Finland was almost double that of the United States and was a subject he had much more expertise in, meaning that I should quit whining about it.

But, I never understood the concept of people having their hands out. I guess that's the difference between a book MBA and a street MBA.

Just today as I'm writing this chapter, I got a call from an associate of mine asking me to speak at a conference.

I enjoy speaking and I enjoy talking to crowds about my passion for Main Street, so I readily accepted.

That is when he wired in a lady who promptly told me that they would be happy to have me there, but that they have a rule that *only members* are allowed to speak.

I said, "That is fine, how much is a membership?" in the back of my mind thinking it would be a nominal, chamber-of-commerce, seventy-five-dollar yearly fee.

And she calmly responded that it was fifteen hundred dollars.

To which I promptly said, "Ouch!"

The "invitation to speak" quickly turned into a shakedown of money from my company for all of the wonderful networking opportunities I would be receiving through the membership.

I passed.

I never realized how many people have their hands out. Everything from the girl scouts, to the little league, to the high school boosters, to the questionable friends of the police department league.

It isn't fun to say no.

We all want to be nice people, but the small business owner who caves into every request for money will not be in business for long—and it starts with your attorney.

Open up your business with the absolute minimal paperwork and licensing.

If you need a physical presence on Main Street, get deferred rent from the landlord.

There's an awfully lot of empty space out there. Don't pay retail. Buy stuff from auctions. Use the hand-me-downs in the attic.

Once you start making a profit, then by all means upgrade.

Your first step as a small business owner should be to demonstrate that you have the ability to generate cash from somewhere.

This may be difficult if you are that Subway franchise, but I would argue that perhaps before you open up your own shop, you partner with an existing owner, and go out and see if you can sell their tray of sandwiches to local businesses.

More importantly, see if you like the business.

Will you have the passion to make sure everything is prepared and delivered correctly, and on time?

That should be your emphasis. Your emphasis shouldn't be on "prettying" everything up when you have yet to know whether you have the ability for someone to write you a check or give you a credit card.

For your product.

And that initial $2,000 that your attorney and CPA wants, up front, could be the difference between success and failure at infancy.

I'll tell you what I did: Initially I operated out of my house. I didn't open a separate banking account for the business for years.

I operate as a sole proprietor. I knew from my banking days that if you have your name on your company, you didn't even have to pay for an ad in the local paper that no one will ever read announcing the name of your new venture.

Remember, the attorney is not your friend. The attorney is a businessman.

Your business model is taking cash from other people. You and he have the same business model, but his model is getting that cash from *you*.

And don't use Aunt Sally's best friend's neighbor. Interview attorneys and CPAs as you would an employee. And only hire those who have an expertise in your field.

Don't trust your banker's referral. They'll just give you names of their customers. My worst experience with a CPA came from a banker "friend." That referral cost me a lot in time and money.

Negotiate a fair hourly rate upfront. Agree to thirty-day terms. Stay away from lump-sum packages of services.

Another trick I used to keep expenses down was to convert all monthly fees into an annual number. All of the sudden, that wonderful service for $19.95 a month that seemed so reasonable becomes $250 a year.

Consider Every Expense Carefully

Do you really need that fancy business card?

To this day, after eighteen years, I still have not bought a copier. That copier that seemed so attractive at $149 a month just didn't make sense at $2,000 a year. After fifteen years that's $30,000 I've saved.

I found out then, and this continues today, that my Main Street has a bunch of people willing to sell me a copy for a nickel.

I thought I was a pretty smart businessman and that I was ready for the recession. But after living and managing through it, I realized I wasn't all that smart.

Consider the price of postage. First we had a Pitney-Bowes machine that was running us about $1,500 a year.

I gave that up for stamps.com, which seemed so reasonable at $15 a month. Even at $180 a year it was cheaper than the Pitney-Bowes machine, so I jumped on the bandwagon.

What stamps.com doesn't tell you (well maybe in the small print) is that you have to buy their labels, and that quickly adds up.

Also, if you make a mistake and print twenty stamps on a blank sheet of paper instead of on their labels, there is no way to recoup the $8.80 mistake. Printing five sheets quickly becomes a $50 mistake. And there is no way to get a refund; another street MBA lesson.

I go to the post office everyday to get my mail; and I've been doing this now for eighteen years.

That was one of the first expenses I had since I worked out the house. Get a real post office box. The cost is around $100 a year. One benefit is you get your mail first thing in the morning.

Another is you want a separate address for some degree of privacy. Don't settle for one of the UPS boxes, because you will end up with some crazy POB street address.

Anyway, as I was fuming over the stamps.com rip-off it finally dawned on me that since I was driving to the post office every day, and I can go anytime I want because I know when there are lines and what time of the month there are lines, then perhaps it would behoove me to buy stamps at the post office.

And I will even take it one step further—not is it only cheaper to buy stamps at the post office, you can now even buy them online. And they will ship hundreds of dollars of stamps to you, for a buck.

So we are back to going old school.

All of our mail now has stamps from the post office and we save a lot of money doing that. And those are the little things that small business owners must obsess about and must understand.

You must be ruthless in saying no and in resisting the urge to get the latest shiny thing.

Frankly, if you're a start-up business, you need to be going with friends or family for a variety of reasons.

The advantage of going with friends is that you want to develop a network of people with a variety of expertise to help you succeed.

Previously we have outlined that the small business owner must be knowledgeable—dare I say even an "expert"—on everything in order to succeed.

The failure to understand a profit and loss statement is as important as understanding the branding for your business or hiring the right person; any wrong move can spell doom for the small business owners.

So I would encourage you to develop an informal board of advisors. You're not going to call them "directors" (for legal reasons) and you're also not going to issue them any stock.

But what you will find along with the line of people with their hands out is the line of people asking for partial ownership.

Consultants are a waste of time, money, and also opportunity cost. If you bring an expert in to help you in an area, the consultant's recommendation will be that if you are successful, that they need to come in and you need to hire them to run the company.

And if you're lucky, they'll only require fifty percent ownership.

I have found in my days as a banker and as a gatherer of small business information, that if you talk to a small-business person, they will readily give up their business plan for free.

You may have to buy them lunch, but it will be the cheapest lunch you ever bought.

I've been in business for eighteen years. One of the keys to my success is that I haven't stopped asking questions. I want to learn about as many different business models as I possibly can. I want to know what works and what doesn't.

One of the reasons people are so quick to give up their business plan is the same reason people talk about their kids: they are proud of what they do.

People have the same pride in their business to where if you ask them open-ended questions, you will be surprised at the depth of knowledge they will give.

That insight is much more valuable than hiring a supposed consultant.

Another reason small business owners are willing to divulge their information is that they understand how difficult their job is.

For many years I was concerned that someone would start to write a rival newsletter and about ten years ago a large company (SNL Securities) did just that.

They folded the venture after a year, but at the time I was extremely worried. I didn't have a clear understanding of the importance of branding, and how important that was in the marketplace.

Oh yeah, when they folded their newsletter they offered it to me first. I did the acquisition with a one-page term sheet. No attorneys, no expenses.

The terms?

I had to fulfill their unused subscriptions with the *Coleman Report*. For overlapping subscribers, I was to issue them a credit. I looked at the numbers and saw I would have to issue about $35,000 worth of credits.

But I would be picking up $75,000 of new business. All I had to do was retain half and I would be ahead of the game, and eliminate a competitor to boot.

But, why no attorneys?

Simple. They had already decided to give up on their newsletter and I highly doubted they would change their mind. And if they did, would I really sue them?

The risk was actually greater on their side. I was the one who had to perform. But they realized the only reason I wouldn't fulfill their remaining subscriptions was if I was out of business.

And if that happened I probably wouldn't have any assets they could recoup from me.

Knowing the motivation of both parties and keeping the attorneys out of it made for a smooth and successful transition for both parties.

Today, I am more than happy to discuss my business model with anyone because I know how difficult it would be for someone to replicate what we've done.

I'm not saying it is impossible.

I am just saying that it takes time and that you have to pay your dues.

There really aren't any secrets. It's all in execution.

Friends

Continuing the theme of friends, when you develop your board of advisors, I would recommend that each of them have a specialization.

They don't necessarily have to have any knowledge about your specific industry, but they should have some expertise in many of the disciplines we have talked about including advertising, sales, marketing, accounting, and legal.

When talking to small business owners and community bankers, I found that people do not understand the difference between *sales* and *marketing*.

Too often these are lumped together. Don't do that. Sales is exactly what it is: bringing sales through the door that you can convert into cash.

The *result* is all that matters.

Marketing is the *process* in which you clearly explain the benefits of your product or service to a potential buyer, moving them from the "Hey that's cool" to the "I need that" bucket.

In my early years, and even up through last year, that has probably been my biggest mistake as a small business owner. I knew in my heart that we provided great service and great product, and we put our product out there because we were so sure people would think it was worthwhile and want to purchase it.

I now understand that I have to present our product in such a fashion that our target banker now says, "Yes, I *need* that information to do my job better."

Our information is sold, not bought.

Venture Capitalism

Bluntly, only one-tenth of one percent of the people reading this book would be eligible for venture capital. I have known several entrepreneurs who have gone the venture capital route, and this is what happens.

First of all the idea must be unique, special, and have the opportunity for wild growth. Traditional Main Street small business is simply not the kind of business that venture capitalists are interested in.

So generally speaking, you are not going to be going the venture capitalist route. But if you are part of that one-tenth of one percent group, then here are a couple of things to remember.

First, do not under any circumstances pay an upfront fee to someone who can "place your deal." If your idea is attractive enough, you will have venture capitalists knocking on your door, not the other way around.

If you are pursuing the venture capital, remember your job is to bring in cash from customers, not from the venture capitalists. That can turn into a full-time job and a full-time nightmare, and will ultimately take away from the chance of success for your business.

If you do succeed in landing venture capital, understand the odds of your long-term employment with the company will be minimal.

You need to do one of two things: Maintain control, which will be very difficult unless you have a proven track record of bringing in cash from your core business; or negotiate up-front your severance package and try to make it as sweet as possible.

Because unless you have 51% control, your blood will end up in the water.

Chapter 14: The Ten Things to Do to Get Your Loan

Now the grand finale. The reason why you bought this book.

Here goes. Here are my tips on how to get a small business loan under the new bank lending models.

There are a number of fine books in the marketplace telling you how to prepare a business plan or a loan package, so we're definitely not going to replicate that process here.

If you want a good reference book on how to prepare the loan package, buy Charles H. Green's book *Get a Small Business Loan – Even with Poor Credit, Weak Collateral, and No Experience*. It's on Amazon.com.

It is an excellent step-by-step guide to all of the documentation items you will need.

It will hold your hand as you prepare projections and other items that you need to satisfy the banking checklist.

I want to discuss the other aspects of getting a loan.

I want to tell you what you need to do that will enhance your chances and minimize the pain of the process.

1) Global Cash Flow Analysis

I know I've laid out a pretty good case why bankers should not use historical cash flow as their number one criteria to make loan decisions, but it is what it is.

You need positive historical cash flow.

You need to understand how the bank will look at your company's historical cash flow. And you better do the calculations for them.

Unfortunately, too many small business owners make their life overly complicated by having many partnerships and different corporations.

If you have succumbed to your accountants and lawyers who wish to fatten their fees, you are one of these victims. The longer it takes for a banker to understand where you generate your cash, the less likely it is you will receive the financing that you will need.

If you are in this situation, you must prepare a consolidated financial statement. Do it for the banker—don't make the banker have to do it themselves.

Next, make sure you understand every line on that balance sheet.

I'm not saying that you need to enroll in an Accounting 101 class in your local college, but I would certainly take advantage of the numerous workshops that a small business development company has to offer.

Also, take advantage of the Service Corps of Retired Executives (SCORE), and pick their brain. Check out your local SBA's website. There's a lot of free training out there. The bonus is that you'll network with others who are going through the same trials and tribulations as you.

Again, there will always be people out there willing to separate you from your cash for their expertise in evaluating and teaching you what you need to know. But you need to be able to know what every line is.

Do not submit anything to the bank that you don't understand. I am not talking about the fraud issues that we discussed in the BLX chapter; I'm talking about your credibility.

For example, let's say that you were showing an accounts receivable number of $250,000, and your sales for last year totaled $1 million.

The banker will assume that dividing $250,000 by $1 million, your receivables (in their jargon) average turn four times a year, or ninety days. That is an unimpressive figure.

You need to be able to explain to the banker that the reason that number is high is because you landed a large contract in the month of December for $150,000, and it has skewed your numbers.

Also, just as you need to understand every line of the balance sheet, you need to understand what every line of your profit and loss statement is.

Spend time with the accountant to clearly understand where the expenses are being appropriated. The accountant is usually there to protect you and minimize your tax liability, and while that is sound and reasonable, tax reporting guidelines are often at odds with banking reporting guidelines.

Now you're going to say, "Wait a minute, according to the CPA rules, everything must be reported the same way." And while that is true, what I am talking about is a level of clarity that makes it easier for the banker to understand your operation.

For example, for tax reporting purposes, all you need to show is cost of goods without breaking them out. But for the banking side of it, it would help the banker's analysis to know what the specific items of those costs of goods are—for example, what percentage are raw materials and what percentage is labor.

Also, you may be renting several different properties to support your business, and while it is perfectly permissible to lump all of that together as rental expense for tax purposes, it would greatly aid the banker's ability to evaluate your business if you separate those out on three line items.

Given the documentation hoops the IRS demands small business owners jump through, auto expense is a tax nightmare.

But, it would behoove you to separate lease payments for separate line items on a profit and loss statement.

Bankers are very concerned with ongoing liability, i.e. monthly lease and rent payments, and a general rule of thumb is to be as detailed as possible when you prepare your profit and loss statements.

Track what is a true auto expense, the truck for your maintenance supervisor, and the car expense you itemize that is really part of your compensation. That's legit to do.

In fact, scour your profit and loss statement and list every personal expense you have the company pay for you.

The banker isn't going to get too excited about whether something is a legitimate expense from a tax standpoint. They'll leave that for you and the IRS to work out.

They want to get a sense of all the expenses you run through the business.

They will also want to know if you have declared all your income.

When it comes to Coleman Publishing I use the takeaway from the first day in Accounting 101 in the MBA program at USC.

The professor said to *always, always account for every dollar of income*. Not reporting all income is fraud.

Then he smiled and said, "Well, there can always be degrees of interpretation of what exactly is an expense!"

I am ruthless on reporting every cent of income. Several times I have been given small gift cards as a token of thanks for a speech. I even report those as income. I'm a little too high-profile in my criticism of the government, so I would be a fool not to.

The bank wants to know what your attitude is on this matter.

The concept of global cash flow is this bottom line: answer the question of how do you make money.

Put it on paper and keep it simple for the bankers to analyze.

Bankers learned their lesson from Bernie Madoff. If your financial situation is so complicated the banker can't figure it out, you are not going to get a loan.

Check out what we've learned from the McCourt divorce trial (they are the couple who own the Los Angeles Dodgers).

They have multiple companies, inter-company transactions, millions of dollars worth of homes.

And they don't pay income taxes.

As I've said, there are only two reasons bankers think if you don't pay income taxes: 1) you don't make money and you don't generate cash, or 2) you're a crook.

Now, if you do this on the advice of your CPA then you need to clearly state to the bank that you really are generating cash, and the accounting shenanigans are legal.

And don't forget that you will also need to convince those banking regulators whom you will never meet.

Oh, and consider this, they work for the same people that the IRS does. Just food for thought as you strategize how you want to handle your taxes.

Now, bankers aren't stupid. They know everyone's sales and profits are down.

There is a simple reason we have record federal deficits and a number of states facing insolvency. Tax revenues are down because business profits are down, and unemployed people don't pay taxes.

But you need to answer the question. Are you someone who lives off loans and debt, or are you someone who can live off your global cash flow?

And if you didn't have cash flow in 2009, or 2010, how is 2011 different in generating cash?

That is the first question you must answer for the bank.

Back to the tax issue. Bankers are reasonable people. They understand the motivation to minimize taxes. It's your job to explain how much cash your business and all your companies generate.

Let me give you a personal example. Specialized Information Publishers Association (SIPA) is a trade group I belong to.

For the past three years I have been fortunate to receive an invitation by the European chapter to come to London and Munich to speak about my business.

My company pays for the trips and I write off the expense. It's a legitimate write-off.

I'm there on business, and I also meet other publishers whom I do business with. I also learn about the new publishing models that will keep me in business. And I have the documentation to back it up.

But I could have turned down the invitation and not spent the money to travel to Europe. This is an example of an expense that could be listed as legitimate cash generated by my company.

2) Off-Balance Sheet Benchmarks

We talked about the five off-balance sheet items that you need to know cold.

I would prepare those as a separate addendum.

It is your job to educate the banker on what the key benchmark items are in your industry.

You'll want to do this for two reasons: First, you want to educate the banker about the sustainability models of your industry, but secondly and more importantly, that you have become an expert in running your business and that you understand how to make money, how to generate cash from it.

And that you are adaptive. You know the new models for your industry.

3) Character is the First C

I've talked about how Google defines your character. You don't need to list personal references anymore. Google does that for you.

Does Google back up that you are you an expert in what you do? Are you managing your online results to back up that you are an expert in your field?

If you Google Bob Coleman, I do OK with images of me on Fox Business News, quotes by other media, and references to my website.

But one of the search engines results for Bob Coleman is the co-creator of a ferret care website, and the author of "How to Prevent Ferret Poop Litter at Home."

I would want the bank to know that's not me. I have nothing against ferrets; I simply don't want to have a discussion about ferret poop. It would be probably to wise to let the bank know that I am pretty focused on what I do and am not putting energy into a venture like this.

Fortunately none of the Bob Colemans listed have been arrested on a scandalous charge.

The point is, do the Google search and answer the questions before the bank does.

Be sure to type in the variety of Google search terms that the banker will use to find out your reputation.

Type in your business, type in your personal name, and understand when that information is out there. If there is something negative, I would mitigate that damage by discussing the topic with your banker before they do their Google search.

It's not just your own reputation that you need to be aware of. Consider if you own, or want to own, a Coldstone Creamery franchise.

You should have an answer for the negative experiences posted on the *Wall Street Journal* blogs from some very dissatisfied franchise owners.

I'm not taking either side in that argument, on whether Coldstones is right or the franchisees are right, all I'm saying is that information is out there and needs to be addressed.

Be aware of all the information that is available on the Internet to evaluate your request. For example, Zillow.com is a website that estimates the value of your residence; and surprisingly, it is very accurate.

If Zillow says your house is worth $250,000 and you value it at $500,000, a red flag will pop up in the banker's mind. If Zillow is wrong, back it up, but realize for a cursory review of values, that is where the banker will stand.

If you are a millennial and applying for a loan, I would simply advise you to take down your Facebook page or at least take it private.

Be prepared to explain any affiliations or organizations you may be a part of. Also, be sure to check more than just the website search; see what comes up under images, under videos, and under news.

If you claim an honor or an award, make sure a Google search will back it up.

They will be able to quickly figure you out from those affiliations. I tell my kids they are identified by the company they keep, and that same concept can be expanded to your business.

You, the business owner, are identified by the groups you affiliate with.

Anything on the web is now permanent. Now more than ever it is critical that you manage your personal branding issues with the same care as you would with your company's branding issues.

What should you do if you don't have a Google presence?

Create one.

Start blogging about your great idea with the intent that you are an expert.

If you want to open a watch repair shop in Yuma, I would be posting articles showing my knowledge, my expertise about Yuma demographics, demand for watch repair services, how I learned watch repair, and oh yeah, how watch repair is my passion.

Write a short article about your concept and release it over the web through a free press release service. I use the web as one service.

Don't let them up-sell you.

It doesn't matter if the *Wall Street Journal* picks it up. You just want it to be in Google Search results.

Do a YouTube video. Interview someone in your field. Search results love videos. If you are intimidated by this, just hire a neighbor kid to get it done. They'll create something pretty awesome for some pizzas.

And this advice is equally sound for the bankers who are still reading the book at this point.

Jobs come and go. Make sure when a potential employer Googles your name, that the results show your lending niche and that you are a small business banking expert in your town.

I banker friend of mine lost his job during the recession.

Unfortunately, the local paper did an unflattering article about the circumstances of his departure. When you Google his name, that's the first thing that pops up.

Use social media to knock that down on the search results, and be proactive. If you don't attempt to mitigate the damage by the article, as Hollywood says, "You'll never work in this town again."

Even though it's the third item on this checklist, character is truly the first C.

4) The Collateral List

In the first or even the second meeting with your banker, you are not going to be doing a document dump on their desk; you will be giving them selected information that if verified will allow them to reach their loan decision: your global cash flow analysis, some financial information, your benchmarks.

But, here are some things you can do prior to the document dump to get ready.

Have someone go through your office and list all of the equipment.

Yes, printers and computer screens with names and serial numbers. Bankers love to have serial numbers so you might as well get this done.

Even if you are applying for an unsecured line of credit.

As I've said, unsecured loans aren't really unsecured. If you default, they have a way to become attachments to your wages at your new job, and become liens on your house.

5) Life Insurance

Some loans may require you to pledge to take insurance as collateral.

Start the process now so you know what the cost is, and more importantly if you're uninsurable, that is something that can be discussed up front and not at the back end.

More importantly, term is really, really cheap! Take care of your family.

6) Embrace the Cloud

Talk to your CPA and make sure you have the best possible accounting system in place.

I personally am a fan of QuickBooks, the online accounting product by Intuit Systems, but I'm sure there are other fine programs out there.

The advantage to having all of your accounting on the cloud is that if the banker asks you a question, you can immediately bring it up on your mobile device and no matter where you are, you can get an answer.

In fact everything should be moving to the cloud. I run 100% of my business off of it. No matter where I am in the world, I can tell you what my daily sales are, and find the phone number of someone in Pittsburgh from my database.

Trust me, when you meet your banker nothing will be more impressive as when you pull up your monthly sales to date off your iPad.

7) Credit Score

I didn't talk about credit scores under character, probably because I don't believe credit scores accurately reflect character, but that is my personal bias. But credit scores are key and I am talking about them here.

First, you can get a free copy of your credit score from the three major credit companies. Go over that and understand clearly each item. If there are derogatory items that aren't yours, obviously get rid of them.

More problematic are the accurate derogatory items that need to be addressed. Do not fall for the clean-up-your-credit-score scams, which are centered around you sending letters denying every item on the credit scores; those are not long-term fixes.

If there is anything derogatory (a collection account, a lien), this should be fully and adequately explained to the lender in a separate addendum.

Document how any hiccups have been paid.

If you just absolutely refused to pay that $500 bill from the plumber when he flooded the house, but he still sent it to collections, I would provide the bank with all of that supporting documentation.

You probably even will want to bite the bullet, settle it, and at least move it from the collection-outstanding to collection-account-paid bucket.

Bankers are actually pretty intelligent. They understand you can't be Mother Theresa.

Managing your credit score is important, and while you may not know the black box of what goes into the credit score, you should know how it affects you.

Also understand that banks report their balances once a month to the credit agencies, so even though you may have paid off your credit card and in your mind it is paid every month, in the bank's mind you may be at the top of the line.

8) Plan B

If everything goes to Hell in a hand basket and you are up against the wall, is there a Plan B?

What will you do if you give up?

Document how you will repay the loan. Is it from spouse's income? Sale of the house and moving to Los Cabos? The inheritance when mom dies? Liquidation of the IRA plan? The sale of the prized baseball card collection? Naming to whom you could sell the company on a fire sale basis? Taking a job teaching, but committed to paying off the loan?

This is one of the Cs. Capital resources.

9) The Company Tour

Submitting a loan application has been described as a dating or courtship process. That is not true. There is only one decision maker in the process, and that is the bank.

Oh, you can choose to turn down their offer and go with another bank, but the reality of the situation is that one side is doing the courting and the other is doing the evaluating.

And just as in a dating situation you put your best foot forward, do not underestimate the company tour and your employees' interactions with the banker.

There is a reason why banks have cut back on small business lending to their footprint. They want to be able to see and feel your operation. Another way to judge your character.

A clean, stress-free environment sends a much stronger picture to the bank than a cluttered, frantic, and out-of-control workplace.

Personalize the experience. Give them their own hard hat. Don't give them a visitor name badge—type in their name. Reserve them a parking spot. Put their name on the day's agenda. It doesn't cost a dime to treat them like royalty. It's a no-brainer.

Introduce them to key company employees.

Don't try impressing the banker by rushing through a tour and then taking them to a nice restaurant. Trust me, bankers eat well. They don't need to be impressed that you know the best restaurant in town.

Consider this.

Lay in some deli and soft drinks. Bring in your key employees and spend the lunch hour just talking about your business. The more information, in any fashion, you can provide, and the more transparent you are, increases your chances for success. Make it fun.

10) The Last C, Conditions.

You've given the bank four of the five Cs.

You've convinced them you have the character and the expertise to run the business and pay back the loan.

You've proven the strength of your global cash flow, even if it's buried in the numbers.

A list of collateral has been provided.

You've thoroughly analyzed your capital resources, and where you can lay your hands on cash.

Now for the last C; economic conditions.

The banker doesn't expect you to perform at a higher level than your peers.

They simply want to know if you've considered how the world economic conditions affect your business, and your ability to create cash from your corner of the world.

Can you create and maintain riches from niches?

You will explain to the banker why your Main Street retail shop has stuff Wal-Mart doesn't sell.

Why the manufactured products you produce in your plant can't be outsourced to China.

Why your services you provide can't be outsourced to India.

You will go through the analysis of how Amazon can't sell the stuff you sell and put you out of business.

And explain why someone with a new iPad app won't put you out of business. Or better yet, you will explain your plans for your iPad app.

You will again reiterate why you are in the top 80% of small business survivors. You will explain to them no one can be as successful as you are with your concept.

You will repeat yourself and make the banker fall in love with you. And fall in love with your business.

<u>Money, Money Everywhere - 194</u>

And then, perhaps then, you will get your loan.

Acknowledgements

Most books have a foreword. I chose not to put one in this book. Well, I guess I did, but it's in the back of the book.

I find them insufferable, singing the praises of the author and the topic. And thanking a bunch of people whom I don't know.

While that's great for the author's ego, and for his friends mentioned in print, I get lost in all the self-gratitude.

Oh, I'm going to do it. I've worked too hard and long on this book not to. But it's here, in the back of the book. That way you don't need to waste your time reading a bunch of names you don't care about if you don't want to, but the people I need to mention get a well deserved tip of the hat.

My passion for Main Street evolved slowly.

My first source of income was pure Americana: a paper route.

But my first real job was on Main Street, working for the Old Man at an A&W Root Beer Stand.

Owners of Main Street businesses are the heart and soul of America. They are the country's conscience. They know the difference between right and wrong. They aren't greedy. They are honest. They do the right thing.

I'm proud of my passion.

My first shout-out is for Timothy Seiber. He's the ghostwriter of the book. I guess the industry standard when you hire a ghostwriter is to tie them up with a bunch of non-disclosure statements.

I don't mind letting people know I had help.

I hired him as an intern out of TCU last summer. Since we are a virtual company we have people working for us all over North America, including a freelancer who does work for us in Canada.

Timothy's a good ol' boy from Texas. And, he can flat out write. Thanks for all your hard and good work kid.

Who next?

Gotta go with another kid—mine: Joseph Coleman. He's been working for me full time since he graduated from CU with a major in.... yep, history. He runs the website and does a Woody Allen by showing up on time 90% of the time. :)

From a dad's perspective, it's a blast working with one of your kids. I can't speak for the kid, but when he complains about something not being fair I explain that I'm the Old Man and "I....... don't.......care!"

We have over 20,000 people who subscribe to our daily email newsletters, so it would be impossible to acknowledge them individually, but I can thank them as a group. Without your support we wouldn't be able to advocate for small business.

Thanks to Thomas Hauk for proofreading and editing the final draft.

Thank you to Deborah Weirick for cover copy, layout, typesetting and help throughout the process.

Now to the villagers who helped with the concept of the book.

Thanks to Larry Hardee who kept encouraging me to write this book. His motivation was pretty strong—if I didn't do it, he said he would take the idea and do it himself!

Thanks to Chris Hurn of Mercantile Capital, the best SBA loan marketer in the business.

Nods to Charley Shumaker, Mike Mutal, Nathaniel Booker, Dr. Gregg Wilkerson, George Porter and Mike Manly.

And of course Paper-Clip's Andy McLaughlin. One of the smartest marketers in the world. Thanks for all your support and encouragement, bro.

I appreciate the professionalism of the small business media on two levels. One, they produce top-notch small business reporting. Second, they give me a little exposure, which I sincerely appreciate.

Thanks to my friends at Fox Business News who have given me the chance to be a voice of small business. Thanks to the producers and the on-air talent who have been gracious enough to invite me talk about my passion—Dagan McDowell, Tracy Byrnes, Gerri Willis, and Connell McShane.

Poppy Harlow of CNN gave me my first TV interview—thanks!

And thanks to some great small business journalists in the print media. Robb Mandelbaum of the *New York Times*, Emily Maltby of the *Wall Street Journal*, CNN's Cat Clifford, Kent Hoover of *Business Journals*, and Bonnie McGreer of *American Banker* to name a few.

I've talked to hundreds of small business owners all across the country as background for this book. Don't have room to name them all but have to acknowledge La Cañada's Kevin Finch, Dave Bobzan, Eric Ovenespour, Andre Nazarian, and Mariam Gotanian.

I've covered SBA's lending programs for over eighteen years. I've talked to hundreds, if not thousands of SBA employees and I thank all of you for your input.

At the risk of ruining their careers I have to acknowledge some of them and publicly thank them for their assistance to me and their professional dedication to serving America's small businesses. I'm leaving out a number of people, but I have to keep the list short.

Miami's John Dunn, Alberto Alvarado out of Los Angeles, Washington D.C.'s John Miller, Jess Knox, Jim Hammersley, Mike Stamler and Grady Hedgespeth, Deputy Administrator Steve Smits, Herndon's Vanessa Piccone, Maine's Moe Dube, and Fresno's Joel Stiner; thanks all.

Now for the hard one. The industry. I know I've forgotten some. I apologize in advance for forgetting your assistance. Most of my background material comes from your correspondence.

But these are the people who had an important part in their ideas in helping write the book. Sincere thanks to Tom Wallace, Geoff Seiber, Vicki Beaudry, Paul Merski, Ami Kassar, Rob Herrick, Judy Canales, Suzy Granger, Pam Davis, Scott Mortland, Brendan Harper, Mike Rozman, Mike Thomas, Karen Bean, Brian Carlson, Kurt Chilcott, Neil Sokoler and Robyn McGloin.

A nod in memory of John Schulte.

Now for the fun one. Thanks to the Empire on Kilrogg for their encouragement; Crumbles, Huskers, Ammanas, Firemonkey, Ayeta, Ambea, Tirren, Rext and Kipperlugs. Most reading this will have no idea what I am talking about and that's OK. Those that know, "For the Horde!"

I've decided to include the story of how I wrote this book. I think it's a little self-indulgent, but everyone I talked to was fascinated with my process, so here goes. Perhaps it will help someone else check off that item on their bucket list.

Getting started was easy. I have eighteen years of newsletter archives. That formed the outline.

Next, I dictated to Timothy. We set up a conference call via Go-To Meeting and he was able record the call through that platform.

Now here's the crazy part. Dictating while sitting at a desk didn't work for me. My ADD would kick in and I would get easily distracted. So I started pacing around the office. I used a Bluetooth headset to make it easier. Eventually, that expanded where I was talking and walking around the neighborhood. Talk about multi-tasking! Working and exercising at the same time.

I'm sure some of the neighbors were ready to have me committed, wanting to know who this crazy guy was walking around in the morning talking to himself!

We got the project to the point where Timothy was able to organize the material into chapters.

We met several times face to face, he coming to Southern California and me going to Ft. Worth. We had it all mapped out, but I needed to put in some major hours cranking out copy. And I couldn't get it done one hour here and one hour there.

There were too many distractions at home, so I decided to find a hotel room, lock the door, and do some serious writing.

I needed to go someplace that was far enough away that I couldn't give up and come home in a day.

That meant flying. I decided to go at the last minute between Christmas and New Year's. I checked airfares. Montana seemed a logical secluded place. But airfares were over $1,000. Alaska? $1,200. Ouch.

OK, back east. D.C. and Florida were over $1,000.

I could fly to Europe for that, I groaned.

So I did.

Actually for less, a lot less.

I ended up booking a round trip ticket to Ireland for $734 with twenty-four hours' notice!

Money, Money Everywhere - 200

I reserved a hotel room for 105 euros a night and off I went.

I pack extremely light. Just one set of clothing was packed. No checked luggage. One set of clothing was worn while the other was being cleaned. I just rotated the clothes like that.

Getting on a plane and getting out of town was the best decision I made in writing the book. I was able to finish out most of the book in those five days.

Here's how I did it.

Flying across the water screwed up my internal clock, so I didn't have any preconceptions when I should sleep and when I should work.

I woke up early, usually 3:00 am or 4:00 am. I would write in the hotel room until 7:00 am. I did my best writing then. I was able to crank out a lot of copy.

The best part was while I was 5,000 miles away, I was wired in with the family and the business at all times.

There is a five-hour time difference to the East Coast and eight-hour time difference to the West coast.

While I wrote early in Europe, America slept. My cell phone was on but no one called. I took emails but those that arrived during that time were simply spam that I trashed.

At 7:00 am I went to breakfast. Now, Ireland in January is *cold*! Fortunately for Christmas my wife gave me a nice warm long overcoat and a great scarf for traveling to the East Coast. That came in handy.

It was still dark, but I went and had a nice Irish breakfast of eggs, Irish bacon, sausage, potato, beans, and bread. And two pots of tea. I've become a full-fledged tea convert.

I did all my writing on the iPad with the Pages app. I have a wireless Apple keyboard and the setup works like a laptop computer, but it's so much more user friendly.

Just to make sure I didn't lose anything, I always send myself an email of the latest version. Bam. Backed up on the cloud.

I would continue to write from 7:00 am to 9:00 am at the cafe and then head back to the hotel.

I chose the Brooks Hotel because that's the name of my dad and kid, and it had an "old school" library in the basement. I would hang out there and write until around 1:00 pm.

That would be seven to eight hours of pure writing.

1:00 pm is significant because that's 8:00 am East Coast time. That's also the time we send out our first email of the day, Coleman's SBA Daily, which Joseph would produce the evening before hand.

At 1:00 pm I would go to lunch.

At lunch, I took a break from writing and worked through the early morning emails.

After lunch I would walk the streets of Dublin and geocache, usually for an hour.

I never did any tourist stuff. I knew the trip was expensive and that worked in my favor. I was determined not to waste any time. I was either writing, eating, walking, or sleeping.

One cool thing is while I walked around Dublin I took a couple of calls on my phone. No one knew where I was and it was just business as usual.

I'd be back to the hotel around 3:00 pm and would get caught up on the emails. Now it was 10:00 am in New York, but the West Coast still wasn't working.

So, a perfect time for a nap! I kept it to about ninety minutes and would be back at it by 5:00 pm.

Except this time I hit the pub downstairs, fired back up the iPad. I kept up on the emails, answered the phone, drank a little Guinness, and polished the book.

I would be at the pub from 5:00 to 7:00 pm Irish time, which was noon to 2:00 pm Eastern and 9:00 am to 11:00 am on the west coast.

The schedule couldn't have been better for producing a ton of writing and keeping up with the business obligations.

Around 8:00 pm, or 3:00 pm Eastern and noon Pacific, I went to dinner. By now everything was usually under control and I spent dinner polishing what I had written that morning and preparing an outline for the next day's output. And I would take calls as they came in.

By 10:00 pm Irish time the East Coast was going home at 5:00 their time and the Pacific coast was starting to wind down at 2:00 pm their time.

I would be in bed by 11:00 pm.

Of course I had a little selling to do to my wife. When I told her what a great schedule I had, that I was able to write over twelve hours a day, keep up with the business, and when I wasn't writing that I was just eating sleeping, or walking, she smirked and pointed out I could do that at home!

I flew home, sent the manuscript over to Tim, who did a nice job of cleaning up a couple of chapters.

The book sat in the computer for three weeks in February when I decided I had to get away again.

I repeated the cycle, this time to Edinburg, Scotland, but for only three days.

And that is how I finished *Money, Money Everywhere—And Not a Drop for Main Street.*

All errors of commission and omission are 100% mine, no excuses up front.

That said, I hope you enjoy the book as much as I did writing it.

Cheers!
Bob Coleman
June 2011
La Cañada Flintridge, California
bob@colemanreport.com

Index

Publications

Companies

People

Money, Money Everywhere - 210

David Chadwick, 21
Davis, Pam, 198
Deaibes, Imad, 162
Dube, Moe, 198
Dunn, John, 198
Finch, Kevin, 102, 197
Gotanian, Mariam, 197
Hamburger, John, 113
Hammersley, Jim, 198
Hardee, Larry, 196
Harlow, Poppy, 197
Harper, Brendan, 198
Harrington, Patrick, 150, 153
Hauk, Thomas, 196
Hedgespeth, Grady, 198
Herrick, Rob, 198
Hoover, Kent, 197
Hurn, Chris, 197
Kassar, Ami, 198
Knox, Jess, 198
Lazenby, Deborah, 156
Lukaski, Debra and Joe, 55
Maltby, Emily, 197
Manly, Mike, 197
McDowell, Dagan, 197
McGloin, Robyn, 198
McGreer, Bonnie, 197
McLaughlin, Andy, 197
McShane, Connell, 197
Merski, Paul, 198
Miller, John, 198
Mortland, Scott, 198
Murphy, Annemarie, 58, 75
Mutal, Michael, 100, 139
Nazarian, Andreh, 20
Oshoff, Richard, 93
Ovanespour, Erik, 20, 197
Patidar, Sherwin, 55
Piccone, Vanessa, 198

9 780983 381174